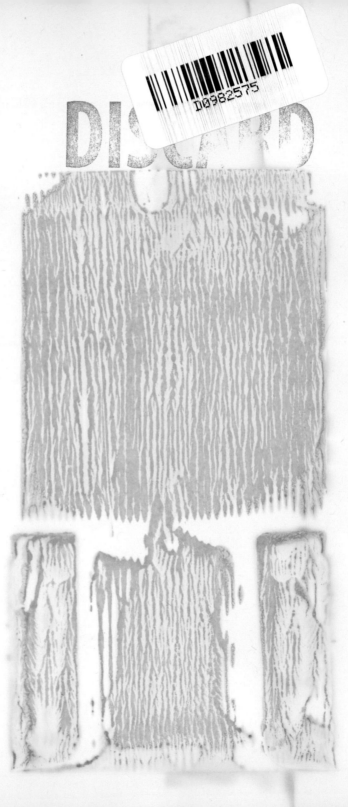

# Economics of Academic Libraries

# Economics
# of Academic
# Libraries

Prepared for
Council on Library Resources

by MATHEMATICA, INC.:

William J. Baumol
and
Matityahu Marcus

AMERICAN COUNCIL ON EDUCATION • Washington, D.C.

© 1973 by American Council on Education
One Dupont Circle, Washington, D.C. 20036

Second printing 1974

Library of Congress Cataloging in Publication Data

Baumol, William J
    Economics of academic libraries
    1. Libraries, University and college—United States.
2. Library finance—United States.        I.    Marcus,
Matityahu, 1934—      joint author.    II.  Council on
Library Resources.    III.  Mathematica, inc., Princeton,
N.J.   IV. Title.
Z675.U5B34              025.1'1              73-10244
ISBN 0-8268-1257-0

Printed in the United States of America

# Contents

# Figures

# Tables

vii

# Preface

This volume represents what we believe to be as complete and thorough an analysis as possible of the available economic data on college and university libraries. In the course of our study, we have examined the data for comprehensiveness and consistency; we have investigated their intertemporal behavior, both as a basis for projection and as an instrument for long-range planning; and we have constructed a set of analytic interrelationships which permit us to derive statistical estimates of the interrelations of some of the most critical economic variables relating to library operations. In particular, in the course of this last step, we have provided relationships explaining statistically the determination of such variables as the size of libraries' budgets and the magnitude of their professional staffs.

It is hoped that the results of our analysis will prove helpful at a number of levels. They can be used by individual librarians in making plans for their own institutions, by college and university administrators in anticipating the future fiscal needs of their libraries and evaluating the financial consequences of decisions on overall institutional policy, and by organizations representing librarians in making their case for the resources they need and determining lines of research that will be most useful in planning for the future.

We should underscore the fact that this study has been limited to the available statistical data and has not attempted to probe into the various nonstatistical elements that also affect the economics of library operations. Factors such as emphasis upon highly specialized research programs, development of completely new fields of educational interests, or efforts to serve as a national or state resource in a particular subject field can have significant effects upon the economics and operations of academic libraries. Although we have attempted in this report to describe specifically some procedures that can be followed in obtaining statistical guidance in the construction of budgets, we are well aware of the other elements that are important in determining the individual natures of different libraries and their special needs and services.

Two different sets of data have been used in this study. Statistics from a special group of research libraries were studied in the chapter 1 analysis of growth rates. Data collected by the Office of Education on a much wider scale were used for chapter 2, "Library Costs in 678 Four-Year Colleges and Universities, 1967 and 1968."

This report is divided into five chapters dealing with different elements of the study. The first describes the results of our analysis of trends and growth rates in the variables examined. The second reports the results of our study of the interrelationships among the pertinent variables, such as the effect of a difference in the size of student body on the overall budget, simultaneously taking into account the influence of other variables. The third chapter is an essay on the longer-term implications of our results for the nature of library operations. The fourth chapter reviews the available data and considers how the bank of information might be improved in the future in light of our experience with this study. Finally, the concluding chapter is devoted to a summary of our results and the ways in which they can be used. Obviously, any such abbreviated listing must unavoidably provide only a general overview of the variety and range of our conclusions. Yet we hope this chapter will nevertheless be useful to the reader as a guide to the report and an indication of the parts that may be most pertinent to his particular needs.

Invariably, completion of a piece of research and its publication take more time than originally planned. This report was no exception. It came as no surprise, therefore, that toward the end of our work somewhat more recent data became available. Naturally, we considered revision of our calculations to take this newer information into account, particularly since the more current materials undoubtedly contain the first manifestations of the new era of financial stringency, which will almost certainly bring with it significant changes in the pertinent financial trends.

After careful consideration, we decided, however, that return to additional calculations was not warranted. One year's additional data can make only a marginal difference to calculations based on figures for two decades. Nor does one have the choice of dealing with a briefer period by ignoring earlier figures since the information is then likely to become inadequate for significant statistical analysis. Moreover, there was no indication that any substantial modifications in our cross-sectional results could be expected.

We concluded, therefore, that revision of our work should be postponed until still more information for the current decade is accumulated. Particularly if our analysis proves to be used widely, a regular periodic revision will be fruitful.

Before closing our preface, we must express our gratitude to the Council on Library Resources for its support of our work and our debt to the advisory council appointed by the council to help guide us in this study. The members of this group were William S. Dix, university librarian at Princeton University, Warren J. Haas, university librarian at Columbia University, and W. Carl Jackson, director of libraries at the Pennsylvania State University. In addition, we have had invaluable suggestions from Fred C. Cole, F. E. Mohrhardt, and C. M. Spaulding of the Council on Library Resources. All of them have contributed time and thought to this study in generous measure, and we have benefited greatly from their help. We trust the results of our study will prove useful and illuminating to those who must deal with the difficult economic problems of the libraries of our nation's colleges and universities.

WILLIAM J. BAUMOL

MATITYAHU MARCUS

# Growth Rates in Fifty-eight Large University Libraries, 1950-69 | 1

The expansion of library holdings, budgets, and other related variables during the postwar period is well known. One of our tasks was to determine the magnitudes of these rates of expansion and to analyze their interrelation in order to provide a guide for future planning and budgeting and an aid to analysis. For this purpose, we employed data for the two postwar decades from 1950 to 1969, for university research libraries.[1] Our sample of libraries at fifty-eight institutions comprised those at twenty-three private and thirty-five public institutions. These institutions are members of the Association of Research Libraries, from which the data were obtained.

In examining the trends described in this chapter, one must keep in mind the nature of the period to which they apply. The 1950s and sixties were a period during which colleges and universities were comparatively well supplied with financial resources. The recent financial crisis of higher education is not reflected in the trends reported in this chapter. Yet, the calculated figures continue to be highly relevant, for they show clearly that past rates of expansion in library expenditures, like those of educational institutions in general, could

1. The data were obtained by the courtesy of University Libraries and Audio Visual Center of Purdue University. For a helpful study of trends based on the same data, see O. C. Dunn, W. F. Seibert, and Janice A. Scheuneman, *The Past and Likely Future of 58 Research Libraries, 1951-1980* (Lafayette, Ind.: University Libraries and Audio Visual Center, Purdue University, 1969).

not have been expected to continue indefinitely. They also help indicate where some of the most pressing problems in library financing are likely to be encountered if the period of stringency in higher education continues.

## Categories of Libraries

To examine changes and trends in university library operations over the last two decades, we classified each of the fifty-eight research libraries by growth of collection ("growth rate") and initial size of holdings ("size"). These classifications constitute crude attempts to produce broad categories of libraries differing significantly in qualitative characteristics. Following this approach, the rate of growth of the collection was calculated for each library, and the libraries ranked accordingly (table 1.1). We see that the bulk of the larger, more established libraries fall in the last two columns, corresponding to slower growth. For example, Harvard, Yale, and Princeton are all in the least-growth category, and Columbia, Berkeley, and Johns Hopkins fall into the class of second-lowest growth. On the other hand, the column giving the libraries that grew most rapidly contains no institution generally considered "old-establishment." Thus, some significant differences seem to have been captured in this classification. The calculation in terms of growth class also enables us to judge the interdependence of growth in various library attributes, i.e., whether libraries whose holdings expand most rapidly also grow most quickly in other ways and whether all of these types of expansion proceed roughly in step.

The classification of libraries by size of holdings is similar in its purpose. Table 1.2 categorizes the libraries by size.

## Method: Interpretation of the Figures

All of the growth rate estimates were computed by the method of lögarithmic least squares. The data were assumed

## Table 1.1

### Fifty-eight University Research Libraries Classified by Growth Rate of Volumes Held

(Showing Percentage Increase in 1968-69 Holdings Relative to 1950-51 Holdings)

| Highest-Growth Libraries | | High-Growth Libraries | | Moderate-Growth Libraries | | Least-Growth Libraries | |
|---|---|---|---|---|---|---|---|
| U. of Utah | 351.95 | Indiana | 195.41 | Boston | 123.52 | Northwestern | 89.45 |
| U. of Maryland | 332.49 | Wayne State | 192.19 | U. of Texas | 122.52 | U. of Colorado | 80.23 |
| Pennsylvania State | 286.32 | Stanford | 189.04 | U. of Southern California | 122.24 | Joint University Libraries[a] | 79.01 |
| Syracuse | 280.02 | U. of North Carolina | 177.86 | U. of Iowa | 118.75 | U. of Illinois | 78.79 |
| U. of California, Los Angeles | 253.57 | U. of Notre Dame | 176.53 | U. of Oregon | 116.96 | U. of Pennsylvania | 76.34 |
| U. of Tennessee | 246.11 | U. of Michigan | 172.21 | Johns Hopkins | 114.14 | Princeton | 75.99 |
| Texas A&M | 224.72 | Rutgers | 168.95 | U. of Pittsburgh | 111.39 | U. of Minnesota | 74.63 |
| U. of Oklahoma | 224.38 | Temple | 166.31 | U. of Kentucky | 111.22 | Brown | 71.63 |
| Michigan State | 219.70 | U. of Wisconsin | 163.81 | Washington U. (St. Louis) | 110.49 | Iowa State | 71.13 |
| Purdue | 217.57 | Ohio State | 147.60 | U. of California, Berkeley | 108.32 | U. of Cincinnati | 61.76 |
| U. of Kansas | 207.31 | MIT | 143.52 | Columbia | 107.26 | U. of Chicago | 53.25 |
| U. of Florida | 202.33 | U. of Virginia | 142.28 | U. of Rochester | 101.96 | Harvard | 45.92 |
| Louisiana State | 198.44 | New York | 134.88 | U. of Missouri | 97.73 | Yale | 34.43 |
| Florida State | 198.00 | U. of Washington | 132.43 | Duke | 96.02 | Washington State | 29.05 |
| | | Cornell | 128.16 | U. of Nebraska | 95.27 | | |

[a] Includes libraries of George Peabody College for Teachers, Scarritt College, and Vanderbilt University.

## Table 1.2

### Fifty-eight University Research Libraries Classified by Size of Holdings, 1950-51

| Large Libraries | Medium-Large Libraries | Medium-Small Libraries | Small Libraries |
|---|---|---|---|
| U. of California, Berkeley | Brown | U. of Southern California | Boston |
| U. of California, Los Angeles | Duke | U. of Cincinnati | Florida State |
| U. of Chicago | U. of Iowa | U. of Colorado | Iowa State |
| Columbia | Johns Hopkins | U. of Florida | U. of Maryland |
| Cornell | Louisiana State | Joint University Libraries[a] | U. of Nebraska |
| Harvard | U. of Missouri | U. of Kansas | U. of Notre Dame |
| U. of Illinois | New York | U. of Kentucky | Pennsylvania State |
| U. of Indiana | U. of North Carolina | MIT | Purdue |
| U. of Michigan | Northwestern | Michigan State | U. of Rochester |
| U. of Minnesota | Ohio State | U. of Oklahoma | Syracuse |
| U. of Pennsylvania | U. of Texas | U. of Oregon | Temple |
| Princeton | U. of Utah | U. of Pittsburgh | U. of Tennessee |
| Stanford | U. of Virginia | Rutgers | Texas A&M |
| Yale | U. of Washington | Washington U. (St. Louis) | Washington State |
| | U. of Wisconsin | Wayne State | |

[a]Includes libraries of George Peabody College for Teachers, Scarritt College, and Vanderbilt University.

to approximate a constant annual percentage rate of growth. The least squares method selects that curve from among the members of the family of constant growth curves which yields the smallest number for the sum of the distances between the selected curve and the dots representing the statistics. The distances are squared to eliminate minus signs. Thus the least squares calculations determine which growth rate curve best represents the actual data.

**Figure 1.1**

**Computation of Growth Rate by Logarithmic Least Squares**

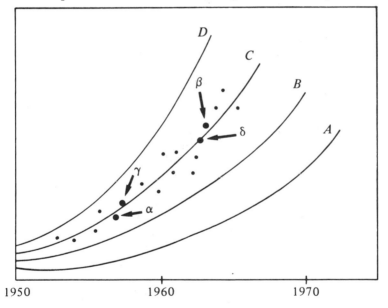

In figure 1.1 any one of the four curves shown has the characteristic shape of a steady percentage growth graph. However, only the curve labelled *C* lies close to the dots that represent the statistics, and thus it is the curve chosen to represent the growth rate under study.

Of course, it is always possible that the assumption of a constant percentage growth rate simply does not correspond with the facts. None of the curves then would follow the pattern of the dots closely. To test for this possibility, one utilizes a concept, the $\bar{R}^2$, which measures the percentage of the variation in the statistical figures accounted for by the movement of the selected curve. For example, note in figure 1.1 that the dots labeled $a$ and $\beta$ are quite a distance apart. But the curve $C$ accounts for virtually that entire difference. That is, if we attribute the move along the curve from $\gamma$ to $\delta$ to the growth process represented by the curve, then only the small distances $a$ to $\gamma$ and $\beta$ to $\delta$ remain to be explained. An $\bar{R}^2$ of 1.00 would mean that 100 percent of the observed variation is explained by the growth hypothesis (i.e., that all the dots representing the statistics actually fall on curve $C$) while, for example, the figure $\bar{R}^2 = 0.95$ means that the dots lie extremely close to the curve. In the two tables that follow (tables 1.3 and 1.4), growth rates with high $\bar{R}^2$ values are identified by one or more asterisks. Any figure without an asterisk should be considered suspect because the actual time path of the corresponding variable did not exhibit anything closely approximating steady growth, and therefore the interpretation of an average growth figure becomes rather questionable.

The interpretation of the numbers in tables 1.3 and 1.4 is perfectly straightforward. These tables simply represent, for each category, the compound percentage growth rates averaged over the two decades which our statistics span. For example, in table 1.3, we see from the second row and last column that in the set of libraries with lowest growth, the number of volumes held increased at an annual rate of 2.6 percent compounded. The triple asterisk after the 2.6 indicates that the $\bar{R}^2$ was higher than 0.95, i.e., that the data really do exhibit a time path very closely approximating a constant growth curve, and the 2.6 figure represents the observed patterns extremely closely.

Several growth rate categories in our tables consistently exhibit low $\bar{R}^2$ values—for instance, volumes held per stu-

## Table 1.3

### Annual Percentage Growth Rates of Various Library Statistics, 1950-51–1968-69, for Fifty-eight University Research Libraries, Grouped by Growth Rate of Holdings

| | All Libraries | Libraries with Highest Growth | Libraries with High Growth | Libraries with Moderate Growth | Libraries with Lowest Growth |
|---|---|---|---|---|---|
| 1. Total enrollment | 4.4** | 6.2*** | 4.3*** | 3.2* | 4.1** |
| 2. Volumes held | 4.2*** | 6.7*** | 5.3*** | 4.1*** | 2.6*** |
| 3. Volumes held per student | -0.2 | 0.5 | 0.9 | 1.0 | -1.5 |
| 4. Volumes added | 6.6*** | 7.1** | 7.8*** | 6.2** | 5.5* |
| 5. Volumes added per student | 2.2 | 0.9 | 3.5 | 3.0 | 1.4 |
| 6. Total personnel | 5.3** | 6.6*** | 6.2*** | 4.3** | 4.4* |
| 7. Professional staff | 3.8** | 4.7*** | 4.1** | 3.7** | 3.2 |
| 8. Professional staff as percentage of total personnel | -1.4** | -1.9* | -2.1** | -0.7 | -1.3** |
| 9. Nonprofessional staff | 6.3** | 8.1*** | 7.9** | 4.8* | 5.3** |
| 10. Total library expenditures | 10.5*** | 11.3*** | 11.1*** | 10.0*** | 9.9*** |
| 11. Expenditures per student | 6.1*** | 5.0** | 6.7*** | 6.9*** | 5.8*** |
| 12. Salaries and wages | 9.7*** | 10.6*** | 10.4*** | 9.2*** | 9.0*** |
| 13. Salaries and wages as percentage of total expenditures | -0.8 | -0.7 | -0.7 | -0.8 | -0.8 |
| 14. Book expenditures | 11.4*** | 11.9*** | 11.9*** | 11.5*** | 10.4*** |
| 15. Book expenditures as percentage of total expenditures | 0.9 | 0.6 | 0.9 | 1.5 | 0.5 |

*Note:* Growth rate was the coefficient $b$ in a regression equation of the form $\log y = a + bt$.

\*$0.85 \leqslant \bar{R}^2 < 0.90$
\*\*$0.90 \leqslant \bar{R}^2 < 0.95$
\*\*\*$0.95 \leqslant \bar{R}^2$

## Table 1.4

### Annual Percentage Growth Rates of Various Library Statistics, 1950-51–1968-69, for Fifty-eight University Research Libraries, Grouped by Size of Holdings, 1950-51

| | All Libraries | Large Libraries | Medium-Large Libraries | Medium-Small Libraries | Small Libraries |
|---|---|---|---|---|---|
| 1. Total enrollment | 4.4** | 3.6** | 4.4** | 4.5** | 5.5*** |
| 2. Volumes held | 4.2*** | 3.5*** | 4.7*** | 4.6*** | 5.4*** |
| 3. Volumes held per student | -0.2 | -0.1 | -0.2 | 0.1 | -0.1 |
| 4. Volumes added | 6.6*** | 6.4*** | 6.9** | 5.8** | 8.1** |
| 5. Volumes added per student | 2.2 | 2.8* | 2.4 | 1.3 | 2.6 |
| 6. Total personnel | 5.3** | 4.5** | 5.2** | 6.2*** | 6.8** |
| 7. Professional staff | 3.8** | 3.4** | 3.7** | 4.6*** | 4.4** |
| 8. Professional staff as percentage of total personnel | -1.4** | -1.1 | -1.4** | -1.6** | -2.4** |
| 9. Nonprofessional staff | 6.3** | 5.3** | 6.2** | 7.4*** | 8.6*** |
| 10. Total library expenditures | 10.5*** | 9.8*** | 10.7*** | 11.0*** | 11.7*** |
| 11. Expenditures per student | 6.1*** | 6.2*** | 6.2*** | 6.6** | 6.1** |
| 12. Salaries and wages | 9.7*** | 9.3*** | 9.6*** | 10.5*** | 10.7*** |
| 13. Salaries and wages as percentage of total expenditures | -0.8 | -0.5 | -1.1 | -0.6 | -1.0 |
| 14. Book expenditures | 11.4*** | 10.2*** | 12.1*** | 11.6*** | 12.9** |
| 15. Book expenditures as percentage of total expenditures | 0.9 | 0.4 | 1.4 | 0.6 | 1.2 |

*Note:* Growth rate was the coefficient $b$ in a regression equation of the form $\log y = a + bt$.

\* $0.85 \leqslant \bar{R}^2 < 0.90$
\*\* $0.90 \leqslant \bar{R}^2 < 0.95$
\*\*\* $0.95 \leqslant \bar{R}^2$

dent, volumes added per student, salaries and wages as a percentage of the total library budget, and book expenditures as a percentage of total library outlays. In none of these cases is the absence of a consistent growth rate (low $\bar{R}^2$) terribly surprising, for each of them involves a quotient of two statistical figures. Suppose we have two statistical series growing at somewhat similar rates (say, volumes held and number of students enrolled). Then, if we divide one by the other (number of volumes by number of students, to obtain volumes per student), the process of division itself is apt to wash out any trend elements and to leave primarily the influence of the random components in the two series. This is a rather characteristic phenomenon in statistical analysis, not to be interpreted as a symptom of unreliability.

As a final preliminary, we should note that there are a number of negative entries in the tables. These mean simply that the corresponding variable was declining over the period. In every case, however, the declines were only *relative*, i.e., professional staff increased more slowly than total staff, salaries and wages increased less rapidly than total budget, and, in the very large, very small, and slowest growing libraries, volumes held increased less rapidly than number of students. This set of results illustrates once again the complexities of behavior one is apt to observe when dealing with a ratio measure (i.e., one that is really the ratio of two different variables), such as volumes held per student.

In utilizing the growth rate figures, it may often be helpful to refer to tables 1.5 and 1.6 as a basis for comparison. These give the actual 1968-69 figures for the university research libraries whose growth rates are reported in tables 1.3 and 1.4. They also serve to characterize the eight categories into which our libraries have been classified. For example, the second row of table 1.6 shows that the large libraries, on the average, hold nearly four times as many volumes as the small ones, even though the difference between the two groups in size of student body (first row) is negligible.

## Table 1.5

### Mean Values of Various Library Statistics, 1968-69, for Fifty-eight
### University Research Libraries, Grouped by Growth Rate of Holdings, 1950-51–1968-69

| | Libraries with Highest Growth | Libraries with High Growth | Libraries with Moderate Growth | Libraries with Lowest Growth |
|---|---|---|---|---|
| 1. Total enrollment .......... | 24,391 | 24,227 | 18,300 | 18,992 |
| 2. Volumes held .......... | 1,278,237 | 2,027,681 | 1,692,972 | 2,579,897 |
| 3. Volumes held per student. .... | 52.4 | 83.7 | 92.5 | 135.8 |
| 4. Volumes added ......... | 89,730 | 125,204 | 86,250 | 103,136 |
| 5. Volumes added per student .... | 3.67 | 5.1 | 4.7 | 5.4 |
| 6. Total personnel .......... | 195 | 271 | 212 | 226 |
| 7. Professional staff .......... | 72 | 97 | 78 | 95 |
| 8. Professional staff as percentage of total personnel .......... | 36.9% | 35.7% | 36.8% | 42.0% |
| 9. Ratio of students to professional staff ... | 338 | 249 | 234 | 200 |
| 10. Nonprofessional staff ........ | 123 | 174 | 137 | 171 |
| 11. Total library expenditures ...... | $2,468,653 | $3,363,205 | $2,445,339 | $3,185,155 |
| 12. Expenditures per student ...... | $101.2 | $138.8 | $133.6 | $167.7 |
| 13. Salaries and wages ......... | $1,335,011 | $1,983,198 | $1,469,594 | $1,838,050 |
| 14. Salaries and wages as percentage of total expenditures ....... | 54.0% | 58.9% | 60.0% | 57.7% |
| 15. Book expenditures ......... | $946,544 | $1,148,486 | $810,945 | $1,080,647 |
| 16. Book expenditures as percentage of total expenditures ....... | 38.3% | 34.1% | 33.1% | 33.9% |

## Table 1.6

### Mean Values of Various Library Statistics, 1968-69, for Fifty-eight University Research Libraries, Grouped by Size of Holdings, 1950-51

| | Large Libraries | Medium-Large Libraries | Medium-Small Libraries | Small Libraries |
|---|---|---|---|---|
| 1. Total enrollment | 23,286 | 21,954 | 19,631 | 21,106 |
| 2. Volumes held | 3,680,409 | 1,737,456 | 1,246,919 | 966,589 |
| 3. Volumes held per student | 158 | 79 | 66 | 46 |
| 4. Volumes added | 162,988 | 93,893 | 78,897 | 71,302 |
| 5. Volumes added per student | 7.0 | 4.3 | 4.0 | 3.4 |
| 6. Total personnel | 412 | 204 | 167 | 169 |
| 7. Professional staff | 150 | 73 | 61 | 60 |
| 8. Professional staff as percentage of total personnel | 36.4% | 35.8% | 36.5% | 35.5% |
| 9. Ratio of students to professional staff | 155 | 300 | 321 | 352 |
| 10. Nonprofessional staff | 262 | 131 | 106 | 109 |
| 11. Total library expenditures | $4,956,188 | $2,398,184 | $2,170,645 | $2,025,886 |
| 12. Expenditures per student | $213 | $109 | $111 | $96 |
| 13. Salaries and wages | $3,054,680 | $1,380,356 | $1,189,144 | $1,064,765 |
| 14. Salaries and wages as percentage of total expenditures | 61.6% | 57.6% | 54.8% | 52.5% |
| 15. Book expenditures | $1,505,796 | $874,896 | $800,336 | $825,894 |
| 16. Book expenditures as percentage of total expenditures | 30.4% | 36.5% | 36.9% | 40.7% |

## Growth Rates: Some Noteworthy Results

All the figures in tables 1.3 and 1.4 are potentially useful in budgetary planning and projection. Even those for which the $\bar{R}^2$ figures are low are of interest in this respect because the low value of that measure itself tells us that the variable in question is characterized by *unsteady* growth, i.e., that projections of variables such as volumes added per student are apt to be difficult and unreliable.

Going beyond these overall observations, let us note several growth rate figures whose values offer us particularly interesting insights into the economics of library operation and its trends:

1. *Volumes held.* From table 1.4, row 2, we see that in small libraries, the rate of growth in volumes held has been significantly greater—5.4 percent per year—than that in large libraries—3.5 percent. Moreover, libraries of intermediate size show intermediate growth rates. Thus, all libraries are tending to equalize the size of their collections with the passage of time, the difference between the largest and smallest being eaten away at a rate of nearly 2 percent per year. The differential is, of course, enhanced by compounding.

Whether or not one approves of this trend, indicating regression of large and small libraries toward a common size, it is surely noteworthy. It should be emphasized, however, that this pattern of regression toward the middle is a common characteristic of almost all statistical series.

2. *Volumes added.* The growth rate differential just discussed seems to be accelerating, though not quite consistently by size class. The rate of growth of volumes *added* is, of course, a measure of the acceleration of the increase in size of library collections (i.e., the growth rate of the growth rate). Row 4 of table 1.4 shows that for small libraries, the number of volumes added has grown at 8.1 percent per year while in large libraries, the rate was 6.4 percent compounded. A similar pattern is shown in table

1.3 where the size of highest-growth library collections is seen to have been accelerating at a rate of 7.1 percent while the lowest-growth library figure was only 5.5 percent. Thus, the differential between the growth rates of small and large libraries has tended to increase even further.

Incidentally, the absolute magnitude of the growth rate in volumes added is itself highly noteworthy. The number of volumes added annually has been expanding at a rate nearly equal to 7 percent per year. Over the two-decade period, on the average, the annual number of additions has quadrupled; and at the same rate of expansion, it will have multiplied sixteenfold from its 1950 level in two more decades. Such are the powers of compounding! Later in this report, in an essay on prospects for the future, the implications of this rather staggering expansion for the economics of library operations will be discussed.

An approximate measure of the effect of inflation on acquisition costs is provided by the difference between the rates of increase in book expenditures and in volumes added.[2] This magnitude suggests that over the two decades under examination, prices of acquired materials have been rising at about 5 percent per annum. Corroborative evidence for this rapid price rise is found in the behavior of specific price indices. Prices of selected hardcover books, periodicals, and serial services in 1968 reached levels of 160, 176, and 178, respectively, with 1957-58 prices taken as 100.[3]

3. *Volumes held per student.* Growth rates for this variable have been virtually zero (in fact, slightly negative overall), indicating that the size of libraries has barely kept pace with the size of student bodies.

---

2. It should be recognized, however, that the inclusion in the volumes added category of items such as gifts and government deposits reduces the reliability of the volumes added figure as an indicator of acquisition costs.

3. See "1968 in Review: Statistics, News, Trends," *Publisher's Weekly*, March 10, 1969, pp. 37-44; "Price Indexes for 1968, U.S. Periodicals and Serial Services," *Library Journal* 93 (July 1968): 2621-23.

4. *Professional staff.* While the size of the professional staff has been growing in virtually all categories, it has declined relative to number of students served, to number of volumes held and volumes added, and in comparison with nonprofessional staff. The relative decline has varied inversely with library size, the small libraries exhibiting the most rapid rate of relative decline—about 2.5 percent per year.

5. *Total library expenditures.* The outlays of university libraries showed a tremendous rate of increase, averaging more than 10 percent per year. Thus, over the two decades, outlays increased approximately by a factor of 8. In considering the implications of such a rise for the management of university libraries—a topic we examine more fully elsewhere in this study—one must bear in mind that with library inputs (staff and acquisitions) rising by about 5-7 percent, an 11 percent rate of increase in outlays is not surprising when rising prices and wages are also taken into account.

The rate of increase in library expenditures was greater, the smaller the institution—not surprising considering the higher growth rate in scale of operations of the smaller libraries. This result is confirmed by row 10 in table 1.3, which shows that expenditures in rapidly expanding libraries did in fact expand more quickly than outlays in libraries of slower growth.

6. *Expenditures per student.* This critical figure will be discussed later in some detail. One noteworthy feature of these data is the consistency in their growth patterns (table 1.3, row 11).[4] They range over our various classes of libraries from a low of 5.0 percent in the highest-growth libraries to 6.9 percent in the libraries of moderate growth, a remarkably small variation in a figure which is

4. Though *growth* in expenditures per student fell within a strikingly narrow range, the level of expenditures per student varied widely—by as much as a factor of 10. See Robert B. Downs, *University Library Statistics* (Washington, D.C.: Association of Research Libraries, 1969), table 4.

itself a ratio (total expenditures divided by number of students). Moreover, these figures all have high $\bar{R}^2$ values, i.e., the growth figures shown were very steady. With an average growth rate of over 6 percent, expenditures per student will more than triple over a span of twenty years.

The range of growth rates in library costs per student is just about the same as that of the growth in total educational costs per student over the period.[5] Therefore, library costs, taken as a share of total educational costs, must have remained approximately constant over the period. That is, they represented no disproportionate problem to colleges and universities.

7. *Breakdown of expenditures.* From rows 14 and 16 of tables 1.5 and 1.6, we see that salaries and wages constitute between 50 and 60 percent of total library costs while outlays on publications make up 30 to 40 percent of the total. Between them, they constitute more than 90 percent of total library expenditures. Rows 13 and 15 of table 1.4 indicate that salaries and wages have declined slightly as a share of the total budget and that book expenditures have increased more or less correspondingly, though these growth rates were by no means constant. This result means that despite the rise in cost of library personnel, the cost of acquisitions rose even more rapidly as the combined result of the growth in magnitude of acquisitions and the inflation of their prices.

As already indicated, the systematic evaluation of the most important of these trends will be left until later. The figures, as we have gone over them so far, do not provide any great surprises. Yet, the very magnitude of these figures and their differences will certainly be impressive and in some cases more than a little disturbing, particularly to someone not fully acquainted with the details of recent developments in library operations.

5. See D. A. Bradford, R. A. Malt, and W. E. Oates, "The Rising Cost of Local Public Services: Some Evidence and Reflections." *National Tax Journal* 22, no. 2 (June 1969): 185-202.

# Library Costs
# in 678 Four-Year Colleges
2 | and Universities, 1967 and 1968

In the previous chapter, the trends in various library variables were examined and their relationships to size of collection and growth rate were presented. The data used in chapter 1 were those collected annually by the Association of Research Libraries. This chapter examines the same variables at a given point in time in order to identify the factors which determine library costs and to estimate the magnitude of their effects. More specifically, in this chapter, we examine the factors which appear to explain variations in library costs for a large number of institutions (678 four-year colleges and universities) in a recent year.[1]

This approach complements the time trend analysis in a number of ways. First, by concentrating on a single year, we practically remove the inflationary factor, permitting us to deal thoroughly with the other variables affecting library costs. Second, since this part of the study included a very large number of institutions, it was possible to incorporate additional factors into the analysis and to perform more extensive statistical tests.

The primary purpose of this chapter is analytical. Here we are in a position to evaluate the determinants of the variables

1. The data for this chapter are those gathered by the National Center for Educational Statistics of the U.S. Office of Education for *Library Statistics of Colleges and Universities: Data for Individual Institutions, Fall 1967* and *Fall 1968* (Washington, D.C.: Government Printing Office, 1969). These data are discussed more fully in chapter 4.

whose behavior over time was observed in the previous chapter. This analysis, determining the influence of variables such as size of collection, size of staff, etc., is essential if a study of costs is to be helpful in budget planning and for decision making.

The study yielded a large number of findings. Before turning to a full discussion of the procedures and the results, it may be worthwhile to present here a brief general summary of the more important findings.

1. Statistical models which incorporate library holdings, acquisitions, and staff explain almost entirely the differences in library operating costs among a large number of institutions.

2. Private institutions appear to have more freedom to adapt their budgetary structure to changing circumstances than do public institutions. This freedom manifests itself in several ways. The library budgets of private institutions typically reflect more closely the institutions' expenditures (per student) on nonlibrary educational programs; the budgets are also more consistently related to the size of the library's holdings. Private institutions also permit greater increases in staff with growth in enrollment.

3. Libraries, in both private and public institutions, do not adjust their inputs, i.e., staff and acquisitions, to small or moderate changes in enrollment; only moves from one enrollment class to another are associated with discernible and systematic changes in library operations. The enrollment-related effects we observed were, in any event, surprisingly small in magnitude.

4. Medium-sized and large public institutions appear to be less adequately staffed than private institutions falling in comparable enrollment categories; these differences were primarily attributable to the larger holdings of the private schools and their higher levels of educational expenditures per student. Staff costs, however, were typically lower in private institutions, especially in the smallest (1,000-2,499

students) colleges and universities. This difference is apparently the result of lower compensation levels in these schools.

5. As expected, acquisitions were found to be correlated with size of holdings, with public institutions generally responding more strongly to a rise in holdings. Acquisitions in private institutions also increase with the level of educational expenditures per student. No such relationship was observed for public institutions.

6. Acquisition costs per volume were lower for institutions in the very smallest enrollment group (1,000-2,500 students), but hardly varied among the larger-enrollment categories. In private institutions, cost per volume rises, on the average, with size of holdings; such a relationship was not displayed in public institutions. Surprisingly, the percentage of science books (physical science, biomedicine, and technology) in the holdings did not appear to affect per volume acquisition costs.

7. The classification of schools as universities or colleges has little, if any, effect on library costs when one is able to account for differences in enrollment, size of holdings, acquisitions, and staff.

### The Sample and the Methodological Approach

The analysis encompassed 678 four-year colleges and universities with enrollments exceeding 1,000; the sample constituted almost 80 percent of all institutions falling in this category. The distribution of the institutions by enrollment and status (private or public, college or university) is reported in table 2.1. The institutions not considered—all two-year colleges and all other institutions with enrollments less than 1,000—differ in important respects from the other groups, and we therefore felt that it would be best to exclude them.

The two largest components of library costs are acquisition of library materials and staff salaries and wages. In 1967-68, for example, these two costs constituted about 90 percent of the half billion dollars spent by all college libraries in the U.S. This fact suggests that an investigation which concerns itself primarily with acquisitions and library staffing will explain a preponderant portion of library operating costs.

In the course of the study, we considered and experimented with many factors suggested to us by members of the Council on Library Resources. Not surprisingly, variations in library costs turned out to be largely explainable by relating them to enrollment, type of control of institution (public or private), size of book collection, and level of expenditures per student. As we report below, these factors accounted in most instances for a very large portion of the variation in costs among institutions.

**Table 2.1**

**Distribution of Institutions in Sample**

| ENROLLMENT CLASS | PRIVATE | | PUBLIC | |
|---|---|---|---|---|
| | *College* | *University* | *College* | *University* |
| 1,000-2,499 . . . . . | 282 | – | 66 | – |
| 2,500-4,999 . . . . . | 59 | 8 | 73 | – |
| 5,000-9,999 . . . . . | 14 | 22 | 69 | 14 |
| 10,000-19,999 . . . | – | 16 | 11 | 23 |
| 20,000+ . . . . . . . . | – | 8 | – | 13 |

Because the values of the variables under study are often affected by a number of influences, one cannot rely on simple correlation of variables when seeking to isolate their effects. For example, since staff will generally increase with both enrollment and collection size, one cannot determine the separate effect of either, unless both are considered simultaneously. Multivariate regression analysis is the statistical approach designed to solve this problem, and we employed it throughout the analysis. Because this technique must be understood if our results are to be of maximum use, we turn now to a discussion of regression analysis and will illustrate how the results are to be interpreted and employed.

## Use of Regression in the Analysis of Library Operations

Multivariate regression analysis presupposes a causal relationship between a number of explanatory (independent) variables and one dependent variable. For example, if library staff is *assumed* to be determined both by the level of holdings and by enrollment, regression analysis can be used to determine the quantitative effect of each of these variables. The least squares technique is used to estimate these effects. As explained in chapter 1, the least squares method provides estimated values (coefficients) which are best predictors in the sense that they minimize the sum of the squared deviations of the actual from the predicted observations. Tables 2.2 and 2.3 present typical results for private and public colleges with enrollments over 1,000, respectively. The results of the calculations for libraries in other types of institutions are offered in tables A.5–A.12 of the appendix.

These tables are, at first, likely to seem complex to readers unfamiliar with regression techniques, and consequently rather careful explanations seem appropriate. As an illustration, consider the third column of table 2.2. In the corresponding equation,[2] we set out to explain variations in the number of volumes added among institutions in the sample by relating acquisitions to several control (or independent) variables: number of volumes held, expenditures per student, and size of enrollment. The upper coefficient across from the first explanatory variable, 0.0278 (first row, third column) indicates that one unit change in volumes held was, on the average, associated with a 0.0278-unit change in the level of additions. Since both variables were measured in units of 10,000 volumes, we may expect a difference of 10,000 volumes in holdings to result in an incremental acquisition of 278 volumes. We must emphasize that this figure is an incremental and not an average measure; that is, it indicates the

2. The complete equation has the following mathematical form: Volumes added = $a_0 + a_1$ (volumes held) $+ a_2$ (expenditures) $+ u$; where $a_0, a_1$, and $a_2$ are coefficients whose values are to be estimated (the numbers in our tables), and $u$ is an error term.

effect on the dependent variable (acquisitions) of a given change in the value of the explanatory variable (volumes held). Indeed, the average ratio of additions to holdings in this group was far larger, in excess of 5 percent. But there is really little point in examining *average* relationships of this kind since they do not provide us with the independent effect of the particular variable, which is, of course, the magnitude required for planning. In other words, average ratios represent the combined effect of several factors while the regression coefficient provides an estimate of the independent effect of a single variable. This coefficient cannot, by itself, explain acquisition levels of colleges which differ in other respects besides level of holdings (for example, in enrollment and educational expenses per student) unless their *separate* effects are explicitly taken into account.

Since the coefficient is only an estimate of whatever the true relationship may be, one must obtain some notion of its statistical reliability before it can be used for prediction. A standard statistical measure, the *t*-ratio, is used for this purpose. The *t*-ratio for each coefficient is the number reported immediately below it in the table. The higher this figure, the more confident we can be that even under repeated sampling, the value of the coefficients would not differ much. Although proper evaluation of the *t*-ratio is possible only after examining the appropriate probability distribution, any *t*-ratio larger than 1.7 in the present study can be taken to indicate a normally acceptable degree of reliability. The coefficient is then said to be statistically significant. In the present case, the value of the *t*-ratio exceeds 36; therefore, the coefficient clearly is statistically significant.

The next coefficient in the same equation (second row, third column in table 2.2) is the estimate of the effect of a unit ($1,000) change in educational expenditures *per student* on acquisition levels. It suggests that a difference of $1,000 in educational expenditures per student will result in a difference of 1,249 in new acquisitions, assuming of course that collection size and enrollment are not changed. Once again,

## Table 2.2

### Regression Results for Private Colleges
### with Enrollments over 1,000

| EXPLANATORY VARIABLE | DEPENDENT VARIABLE | | | | |
|---|---|---|---|---|---|
| | Number of Professional Librarians | Total Library Staff | Volumes Added, 1967-68 (x 10,000) | Cost of Volumes Added (x $100,000) | Total Library Operating Costs (x $100,000) |
| Volumes held, 1966-67 (x 10,000) | 0.3478 | 1.3929 | 0.0278 | 0.004 | 0.0531 |
| $t$-ratio ........... | 35.8022 | 20.7189 | 36.5042 | 0.3194 | 21.1494 |
| Expenditures per student (x $1,000) | 1.4881 | 6.3905 | 0.1249 | – | – |
| $t$-ratio ........... | 7.6933 | 4.7746 | 8.2247 | – | – |
| Volumes added, 1967-68 (x 10,000) | – | – | – | 0.7153 | 1.0184 |
| $t$-ratio ........... | – | – | – | 19.4872 | 14.5315 |
| College enrollment 2.500-4.999 (x 1,000) ....... | 2.2598 | 12.9504 | 0.3152 | 0.2058 | 0.2047 |
| $t$-ratio ........... | 2.2807 | 1.8889 | 4.0530 | 3.2824 | 1.8695 |
| College enrollment 5.000-9.999 (x 1,000) ....... | 8.6859 | 27.2886 | 1.0170 | 0.2645 | 0.0234 |
| $t$-ratio ........... | 6.5645 | 2.9805 | 9.7931 | 2.8969 | 0.1455 |
| College enrollment 10.000-19.999 (x 1,000) ....... | 14.0553 | 66.0509 | 2.7906 | 0.2978 | 1.1335 |
| $t$-ratio ........... | 6.9020 | 4.6874 | 17.4600 | 1.8121 | 3.9515 |
| College enrollment 20+ (x 1,000) .... | 23.4637 | 175.4912 | 2.9594 | 0.4512 | 0.3280 |
| $t$-ratio ........... | 6.7577 | 7.3045 | 10.8598 | 1.9416 | 0.8063 |
| Number of professional librarians | – | – | – | – | 0.0568 |
| $t$-ratio ........... | – | – | – | – | 10.2256 |
| Constant term ..... | 0.7082 | –1.7981 | 0.2056 | –0.0506 | –0.3718 |
| $t$-ratio ........... | 1.3758 | –0.5048 | 5.0878 | –1.6438 | –6.8929 |
| $\overline{R}^2$ ............. | 0.9004 | 0.7742 | 0.9238 | 0.9229 | 0.9831 |

*See note on facing page.*

22

the *t*-ratio (8.2247) suggests that the coefficient is statistically significant.

The next group of variables, usually referred to as "dummy variables," is intended to represent the average effect of a given enrollment category on acquisition levels. This effect is calculated by classifying all institutions into one of four enrollment classes and determining simultaneously the effect of membership in each particular group on acquisitions. An alternate approach to the evaluation of the effect of enrollment is to calculate a separate statistical relationship for each enrollment category and then compare the coefficients in the different equations. In our analysis, both approaches have been employed.

When the actual enrollment figures for the institutions were introduced, they did not show a significant relationship to library activities *within* an individual size category. This result indicates that acquisitions, staffing, and total operating costs are not responsive to small changes in enrollment. Only

---

*Note:* Data used for the regression analysis were those gathered by the U.S. Office of Education for *Library Statistics, Fall 1967* and *Fall 1968.* With the exception of the volumes held figures, all data were for 1967-68. The variable definitions which follow are taken from *Library Statistics, Fall 1968,* pp. 169, 172.

*Volume*
    A volume is a physical unit of any printed, typewritten, handwritten, mimeographed, or processed work contained in one binding or portfolio, which has been classified, cataloged, or otherwise prepared for use. Included are bound periodical volumes and all nonperiodical government documents.

*Expenditures per student*
    Total educational and general expenses less total operating expenditures for library, divided by total enrollment.

*Professional librarians*
    Staff doing work that requires training and skill in the theoretical or scientific aspects of library work, as distinct from its mechanical and clerical aspects.

*Total library staff*
    All staff serving libraries in regular positions (that is, full-time or part-time positions functioning at least during the fall term).

*Cost of volumes added*
    Expenditures for books and other library materials.

*Total library operating costs*
    Consist of total salaries before deductions; salary equivalence of contributed-service staff; wages paid to students and other hourly assistants; expenditures for books and materials, for binding and rebinding; and all other operating expenditures.

# Table 2.3

## Regression Results for Public Colleges with Enrollments over 1,000

| EXPLANATORY VARIABLE | DEPENDENT VARIABLE | | | | |
|---|---|---|---|---|---|
| | *Number of Professional Librarians* | *Total Library Staff* | *Volumes Added, 1967-68 (× 10,000)* | *Cost of Volumes Added (× $100,000)* | *Total Library Operating Costs (× $100,000)* |
| Volumes held, 1966-67 (× 10,000) | 0.5465 | 1.6919 | 0.0449 | 0.0015 | 0.0200 |
| *t*-ratio .......... | 22.6188 | 17.7744 | 12.6788 | 0.5384 | 3.0521 |
| Expenditures per student (× $1,000) | 0.5446 | 4.8960 | −0.0202 | − | − |
| *t*-ratio .......... | 1.3547 | 3.0913 | −0.3424 | − | − |
| Volumes added, 1967-68 (× 10,000) | − | − | − | 0.6587 | 0.9826 |
| *t*-ratio .......... | − | − | − | 16.8044 | 14.8332 |
| College enrollment 2.500-4.999 (× 1,000) ....... | 3.2971 | 8.3700 | 0.4133 | 0.2048 | 0.1939 |
| *t*-ratio .......... | 2.0289 | 1.3073 | 1.7351 | 1.3490 | 0.7755 |
| College enrollment 5.000-9.999 (×1,000) ........ | 5.3873 | 10.0149 | 0.9020 | 0.1981 | 0.1479 |
| *t*-ratio .......... | 3.3428 | 1.5773 | 3.8183 | 1.2901 | 0.5819 |
| College enrollment 10.000-19.999 (× 1,000) ....... | 6.0033 | 5.4640 | 2.2789 | 0.5446 | 0.6838 |
| *t*-ratio .......... | 2.5779 | 0.5956 | 6.6766 | 2.3249 | 1.7781 |
| College enrollment 20+ (× 1,000) .... | 32.8283 | 88.8756 | 3.3586 | 1.4354 | 3.3754 |
| *t*-ratio .......... | 9.3777 | 6.4443 | 6.5457 | 4.1074 | 5.9034 |
| Number of professional librarians | − | − | − | − | 0.0947 |
| *t*-ratio .......... | − | − | − | − | 9.7886 |
| Constant term ..... | 0.2309 | −2.9410 | 0.5468 | 0.0311 | 0.0271 |
| *t*-ratio .......... | 0.1775 | −0.5738 | 2.8673 | 0.2776 | 0.1477 |
| $\bar{R}^2$ .............. | 0.8447 | 0.7638 | 0.6974 | 0.8258 | 0.9384 |

*Note:* Definitions of variables can be found in the note to table 2.2 on page 23.

major enrollment shifts from one category to another showed significant effects.

Within the framework of the model which we employed, the enrollment effect for a given size category is the difference between the value of the dependent variable (in our example, the level of acquisitions) for this category and that for the smallest enrollment category. For instance, the coefficient reported for private colleges with 2,500-4,999 students shows that institutions falling into this enrollment category acquired, on the average, 3,152 more volumes than institutions in the smallest (1,000-2,499 students) category. Similarly, institutions in the next group (enrollments of 5,000-9,999) acquired about 10,000 more volumes each than those in the smallest category and, by implication, about 7,000 more than those in the 2,500-4,999 enrollment group. Institutions in the 10,000-19,999 category acquired an amount larger than those in the preceding group by about 18,000, and 27,906 more than those in the smallest group. All these coefficients showed *t*-ratios substantially over 2 and can be considered statistically significant.

The enrollment class effect, as one factor in a multivariate equation, does not take into account the effect of changes in other variables which may typically accompany large enrollment changes. Thus, while in reality an institution's shift from one enrollment class to the next is probably associated with a larger collection size, the effect of the latter on acquisitions must be added on when the total change in acquisitions is calculated from our equations.

All reported equations also include a value referred to as the constant. This value may be considered the level of the dependent variable which will continue no matter what the values of the independent variables, at least within some relevant range. For example, if in order to maintain its quality, a library must continue to acquire $x$ volumes per year no matter what happens to enrollment at the institution, the magnitude of $x$ should be indicated by the constant term.

Statistically, this value must be taken into account in estimating the *magnitude* of the dependent variable (i.e., total acquisitions equal $x$ plus acquisitions resulting from increased enrollment). However, the $x$ value is irrelevant in studying responses—i.e., *changes*—in the dependent variable precisely because it is a constant.

The last term in each column is the $\bar{R}^2$. As discussed more fully earlier, this term measures the percentage variation in the statistic under study accounted for by the variation in the independent variables when these are assumed to exert the influence specified by the estimated coefficients of the equation. Thus, in the equation of the third column of table 2.2, we see that as much as 92 percent of the variation in the level of acquisitions is explained by the variables used in this particular equation.

The regression coefficients have many important uses. At a minimum, they offer estimates of the quantitative interrelationships affecting the economics of university libraries and provide estimates of the net effects of a number of variables that influence library operations.

These effects can be viewed as comparative norms by individual institutions seeking to determine whether they lag behind similar institutions. Of course, one must caution against viewing the results as the standards for adequate library services; they merely reflect prevailing practices.

The regression coefficients can also help the librarian in planning his operation and budgeting. For example, if he has information indicating that his institution plans a 25 percent increase in enrollment, the relevant coefficients will help him in planning the appropriate budgetary response. We return to the subject of enrollment-related effects in the last section of this chapter.

### Library Staff

The role of the college library staff in providing adequate services is well known, if not always fully appreciated. It includes instructional and research activities, planning to

Table 2.4

**Mean Number of Professional Librarians and Other Library Staff**

| ENROLLMENT CLASS | PRIVATE INSTITUTIONS | | PUBLIC INSTITUTIONS | |
| --- | --- | --- | --- | --- |
| | Professional Librarians | Total Staff Other than Professional Librarians | Professional Librarians | Total Staff Other than Professional Librarians |
| 1,000–4,999 ...... | 5.2 | 6.7 | 7.3 | 8.6 |
| 5,000–9,999 ...... | 24.9 | 44.6 | 15.9 | 22.1 |
| 10,000+ ......... | 60.6 | 127.1 | 56.8 | 97.8 |

*Source:* U.S. Office of Education, *Library Statistics of Colleges and Universities: Analytic Report, Fall 1968* (Washington, D.C.: Government Printing Office, 1970), table 15.

meet academic needs for library services, coordination with faculty, planning and management of acquisitions, development of cooperative programs with other institutions, processing of publications, and general management responsibilities. It is therefore not surprising that the quality of library services is strongly related to the size and composition of the staff. From a budgetary point of view, staff constitutes the largest expense category, and hence clearly deserves careful attention in a study of this nature.

The Office of Education distinguishes among three categories of library personnel: professional librarians, other professional staff, and nonprofessional staff.[3] However, our discussions with members of the Council on Library Resources suggested that not all universities adhere to the Office of Education definitions in classifying personnel; this fact must be borne in mind when the statistical results are interpreted.

A look at average size of staff, by type and size of institution (table 2.4), reveals that for institutions with over 5,000

3. "*Professional librarians* are defined as staff doing work that requires training and skill in the theoretical or scientific aspects of library work as distinct from its mechanical and clerical aspects. *Other professional staff* are personnel who, though not professional librarians, are in positions normally requiring at least a bachelor's degree. *Nonprofessional staff* are persons who perform receiving, shipping, storing, and secretarial duties, and similar personnel, exclusive of maintenance staff and students or other assistants serving on an hourly basis" (U.S. Office of Education, *Library Statistics, Fall 1967*, p. 4).

students, private schools employ more professional librarians and other staff than do public institutions. Thus, while some sixteen professional librarians were employed on the average in a public institution with 5,000-9,999 students, for the corresponding private institutions, the figure was nearly twenty-five. In the very large and very small institutions, the mean values for the number of professional librarians do not differ much between public and private institutions. But useful inferences cannot be drawn from such a gross comparison of public and private universities. One must take into account other factors that are likely to influence staff size.

After experimenting with various variables, we found that one can obtain a fairly good statistical explanation of the differences in size of staff by taking into account size of collection, educational expenditures per student, type of institution, and enrollment class. Indeed, these factors explain 90 percent and 84 percent of the variation in number of professional librarians in private and public institutions respectively. (See tables 2.2 and 2.3.) Table 2.4 presents the difference in staff size between private and public institutions after removing statistically the influence of differences in the size of holdings and expenditures per student.

*Size of Collection and Size of Staff.* The regression results suggest that in both public and private institutions, professional librarians and all other staff vary significantly with the size of collection, though not at the same rate. More specifically, for institutions within the same enrollment class and with equal educational expenditures per student, more professional librarians are added as size of collection is increased (tables 2.2 and 2.3). In both types of institution, however, the indicated additions are surprisingly low in absolute value: if the collection is increased by 100,000 volumes, the number of librarians increases in public institutions by 5.5, in private institutions by 3.5.

The impact of collection size on staff *other than librarians* is about the same for private and public institutions: a 10-member staff increase for an addition of 100,000 volumes. We should note, however, that the effect of collection size in public institutions, unlike that in private institutions, was not uniformly significant or stable in value when estimated for the separate enrollment categories. Only at the 10,000- to 20,000-student range do we find public and private institutions exhibiting almost identical values.

*Role of Educational Expenditures per Student.* The level of educational outlays per student was found to influence library staff size, but not in all enrollment categories. No significant effect was established for the 10,000-19,999 enrollment category for either public or private institutions, nor for the 1,000-2,499 category in public institutions; that is, in these cases the statistical evidence is not sufficiently strong to permit us to be confident of its conclusions. With this caveat in mind, one may suggest, nonetheless, that on the average, a given increase in educational outlays per student in private schools would be associated with an increase in the number of librarians three times as large as that shown for public institutions. These data seem to suggest that in public institutions a relatively low priority is assigned to library activities as additional funds are made available for educational expenditures. We will see later that a similar relationship seems to characterize public institutions' acquisition policy.

*Effects of Enrollment Size.* Size of library staff was also strongly associated with the enrollment class in which an institution fell, though it was not responsive to minor differences *within* enrollment categories.[4] The magnitude of

4. In evaluating the significance of the enrollment-related effects, we must consider the possibility that they merely reflect an associated increase in the percentage of universities as one moves to successively larger enrollment sizes. However, the evidence leads us to discount the role of this effect. Separating colleges from universities did not suggest the presence of a consistent or significant difference in size of library staff in three instances (private 5,000-9,999, public 5,000-9,999, and public 10,000-20,000). Only in one group, private 2,500-4,999, did colleges employ a significantly smaller number of professional librarians than universities with the same holdings and educational outlays per student. (An institution was classified as a university if it gives considerable emphasis to graduate instruction, awards advanced degrees as well as baccalaureates in a variety of liberal arts fields, and has at least two professional schools that are not exclusively technological in nature.) See the effect of classification as a college in equation 3 of table A.13.

these enrollment effects, when collection size and educational outlays per student are held constant by statistical means, is summarized in table 2.5. We see that in most cases, with an increase in enrollment, the library staff in private institutions increases by a larger number than that in public institutions. When considering staff members other than librarians, the patterns of response of public institutions are far less regular. This fact seems to suggest that public institutions may not be as free as private institutions to reapportion their total budgets in response to variations in user needs.

Table 2.5

**Size of Library Staff in Institutions
with 2,500 or More Students Relative to Staff Size
in Institutions with Enrollments of 1,000-2,499**

| ENROLLMENT CLASS | PRIVATE INSTITUTIONS | | PUBLIC INSTITUTIONS | |
|---|---|---|---|---|
| | *Difference in Number of Professional Librarians* | *Difference in Number of Other Staff* | *Difference in Number of Professional Librarians* | *Difference in Number of Other Staff* |
| 2,500-4,999 . . . . . | 2.25 | 10.70 | 3.30 | ** |
| 5,000-9,999 . . . . . | 8.68 | 18.60 | 5.39 | ** |
| 10,000-19,999 . . . | 14.05 | 52.00 | 6.00 | ** |
| 20,000+ . . . . . . . . | 23.46 | 152.03 | 32.83 | 55.00 |

*Note:* Data, which are based on regression results in tables 2.2 and 2.4, assume collection size and educational expenditures per student are held constant.

**Estimates were not statistically significant.

The figures in table 2.5 suggest that the effect of enrollment on library staff size is astonishingly small; in public institutions, professional librarians are added at a rate of less than one for 1,000 additional students, except in the few largest institutions (20,000+ students). For example, in the 10,000-19,999 enrollment category (average size, 15,000), there are only six more professional staff members than in the 1,000-2,499 enrollment group. The additions are only slightly higher in private institutions.

## Acquisition of Library Materials

College libraries have been adding to their holdings at a substantial rate; in 1967-68 alone, college libraries in the U.S. added 25 million volumes, or about 8.25 percent of their entire collection. While acquisition policy is in part dependent upon the rate at which new publications appear, there are obviously great differences in acquisition policies among institutions. To determine which variables can account for these variations, we experimented with several formulations but finally settled on the relationship represented by the third column in tables 2.2 and 2.3. Basically, the equation described in this column enables us to identify the separate effects of collection size, educational expenditures per student, enrollment, and type of institution (public or private).

*Effect of Size of Collection.* Turning to specific findings, we first note the relationship between the level of acquisitions and collection size. A difference of 10,000 volumes was associated with a difference of 278 acquisitions for private institutions, when other factors are taken into account. For public institutions, a 10,000-volume difference in holdings produces a substantially larger effect on acquisitions—a 449-volume increase.

*Educational Expenditures per Student.* The degree of budgetary restrictiveness of the institution is undoubtedly also important in explaining the level of acquisitions. One naturally expects schools able to provide relatively generous support to their instructional programs also to acquire a larger number of volumes for their libraries. To evaluate this influence, we incorporated educational expenditures per student (excluding library costs) into the analysis. Generally, the results show that this variable does have a consistent, if moderate, effect on the level of acquisitions. A difference of $100 in educational outlays per student in private institutions is associated with 125 acquisitions, other factors assumed constant. This influence is not as pronounced in public institutions, appearing significant only in institutions with enrollments from 5,000 to 10,000. In private institutions, on the other hand, outlays per student were a statistically significant factor in most enrollment categories. This result suggests the hypothesis, which seems not entirely implausible, that there is a smaller degree of freedom for public institutions in determining how best to allocate their total budgets.

*Enrollment and Acquisitions.* The last influence on the volume of acquisitions to be considered is enrollment. Perhaps surprisingly, we found no relationship between enrollment and acquisition levels *within* any of the four enrollment categories, suggesting that acquisition policies are not affected by small differences in enrollment. However, when one considers differences in acquisition levels across enrollment categories, the picture changes. More specifically, for any given level of library holdings and educational expenditures per student, the higher the enrollment class, the larger the acquisition level. Enrollment effects on acquisitions hardly differ between private and public institutions.

There are probably several reasons why enrollment affects acquisitions. Larger schools are likely to have a greater number of educational programs requiring continuing additions to their holdings. Also, the percentage of universities in the sample increases as we move up to larger enrollment categories, and since universities place heavier emphasis on research, their acquisitions may be larger. The role of this variable was evaluated by incorporating an additional control variable, designation of each institution as a college or university. The results of this analysis were mixed, suggesting that this factor has at best a limited role in explaining the effect of large enrollment changes on acquisitions.

## Cost of Acquisitions

If all colleges purchased the same mix of books, paid the same prices, and had the same ratio of donated-to-purchased materials, cost per volume would differ little from one institution to another. Obviously, these three conditions do not hold, and one does in fact observe a considerable degree of variation in per-unit acquisition costs.

An increase of 10,000 volumes added was found to produce an incremental expenditure of about $70,000, yielding a cost per volume of $7 (the figure is slightly lower for public institutions). This cost increases with size (enrollment class) of institution. Thus, private institutions in the 2,500-19,999 enrollment groups will incur an additional cost of $2-$3 per volume over the smallest institutions. In public institutions the effect of college size on acquisition costs is less consistent.

We may note here what appears to be an important difference between private and public institutions. For the former we found that, *within* individual enrollment classes, acquisition costs increased with the size of holdings. This trend may be caused by a change in the kind of volumes ordered as total holdings rise. It is reasonable to assume that after the most elementary needs are met, libraries would order a greater percentage of more expensive items—research materials, periodicals, and the like. But such a relationship could not be established for public institutions with the exception of the 10,000-19,999 enrollment class. Although we cannot be certain of the significance of this finding, it may suggest that more expensive materials are generally not selected by small and medium public institutions when they expand the size of their collection. This phenomenon may be caused either by budgetary restrictions or by a lesser emphasis on the research role of the library. Specifically, only in the very large public institutions—those with 10,000-19,999 students—do we find acquisition costs to be affected by collection size in a manner similar to private institutions.

### Library Operating Costs

In the previous two sections, we examined libraries' staffing and acquisition levels. Although these functions account for the bulk of library operating costs (almost 90 percent), other cost items are also of interest and their analysis can certainly be useful for budgetary purposes. We therefore turn to the analysis of total library operating costs, an aggregate which reflects all expenditure items.

The model we employed utilizes collection size, level of acquisition, staff, enrollment, and type of institution. A brief explanation why collection size is introduced here is in order. Its inclusion was designed to capture operating costs other than salaries, wages, and cost of acquisitions. Among these are binding, equipment, other operating expenditures, and interlibrary loans. These cost items can be expected to vary with size of collection.

The results we obtained, which will be described presently, suggest that the chosen explanatory factors explain virtually the entire variation of operating costs among institutions (98 percent of the variation of private, and 94 percent of that of public institutions). Therefore, the estimates which the analysis yielded can be viewed with a considerable degree of confidence.

*Size of Collection.* The regression results show that the effect of collection size on operating costs was higher and statistically more significant in private than in public institutions. A difference in collection of 10,000 volumes at private institutions produces on average an additional library expense of about $5,000 annually. In public institutions, on the other hand, the association with collection size is weaker, and the indicated budgetary support rises are considerably lower— only about $2,000 for an increase of 10,000 volumes in collection size. This difference suggests that in public institutions, budgetary support for those functions related to collection size is less consistent and of lower magnitude.

*Acquisitions.* The effect of acquisitions on total library operating costs is very similar; on the average, in both private and public institutions, roughly a $10 increase per year is required for each addition to the number of volumes acquired (per year). This estimate exceeds the figure for direct acquisition costs obtained earlier by a substantial amount, reaffirming the well-known observation that the full cost of a newly acquired volume far exceeds its purchase price since a new acquisition requires cataloging and other types of processing.

*Staff Size.* Some of our more aggregate models indicated that public and private institutions differ in the influence of staff size on total operating costs, with public institutions showing a substantially higher cost figure for additional librarians. Closer examination of the data suggests that this result may not hold for every enrollment category, but may well reflect the disproportionately large number of very small private institutions in the total. In the small private schools, low salaries and a large portion of donated services apparently combine to yield astonishingly low cost estimates for library employees.

When we examine the second size class (2,500-4,999 students), we find that the cost effect of librarians is the same in both private and public institutions. In the remaining enrollment categories (5,000+), public institutions show slightly higher staff-related costs.

*Enrollment.* The relationship between enrollment and total operating costs may appear somewhat surprising. Enrollment and operating costs *within* individual enrollment categories show little correlation, in line with earlier findings that staffing and acquisitions were not significantly correlated with enrollment. Although the correlation improves markedly when all enrollment classes are pooled, the regression results show that the independent effect of enrollment on costs (i.e., any effect apart from the association of enrollment with collection and staff size) is small and not very significant. Very roughly, it is on the order of $10 for each additional student.

The low association between enrollment and total costs does not, upon reflection, appear surprising. For it is only through the expansion of library inputs (staff, collection, etc.) that costs are incurred, and these cost factors are accounted for separately in the model.

## Applications of the Findings to Budget Preparation

The results described so far go beyond the provision of a clearer understanding of the economics of library operations; they can be of direct help in budget preparation and for long-term planning. In this section, we indicate in specific terms how such planning might proceed.

Obviously, no single approach to budget making is likely to meet the particular needs and circumstances of each and every institution. Our discussion will therefore point out a range of procedures, from the very simple to the relatively more complex.

Some institutions may prefer to rely entirely on a time series analysis such as that presented in chapter 1. This is clearly the simplest tool and at the same time fairly reliable, at least in the statistical sense. Consulting tables 1.3 and 1.4, the reader will immediately note that the annual compound rate of increase in the total library budget falls within a very narrow range, between 9.8 and 11.7 percent, depending upon the size and growth category of the institution.

The total operating budget can be broken up into its two most important components: expenditures on staff and on acquisitions. The growth rates of these series are found in rows 12 and 14 of tables 1.3 and 1.4, and can be used with a reasonable degree of confidence. Since the student is one of the primary recipients of library services,[5] when requesting additional funds, some institutions may find it useful to break out explicitly a component that is required merely to compensate for the growth of the student body and a com-

5. Of course, we do not mean to suggest that the number of students is the most significant influence on library costs. The range and type of research programs, the number of faculty, and the distribution of their fields are undoubtedly more influential, but we simply did not have the data to estimate these influences statistically.

ponent attributable to all other factors (improved services, inflation, etc.). In the most simplistic variant of this approach, a school which expects its enrollment to increase by, say, 5 percent per annum would grant the library an increase of 5 percent, *plus* the expected rate of increase in cost per student as reported in row 11 in tables 1.3 and 1.4, as a proxy for the other important components of future requirements.

A more complex, yet somewhat more analytic approach to budget making would utilize both our cross-sectional results, reported in this chapter, and the time series trends discussed in the previous chapter.

As a concrete illustration, let us start with the projection of professional manpower requirements. The first step in such a procedure is to calculate the expected levels of library hold-ings and expenditures per student in the year for which the requirement is to be estimated. Next, one turns to the sta-tistical table pertaining to the group in which the school in question falls (among tables A.5–A.12). Each of the expected values (holdings and expenditures per student) will then be multiplied by its associated coefficient from column 1. The sum of these products plus the constant, also reported in column 1, will yield the required level of professional li-brarians if 1968 service norms are not to deteriorate. To this figure, one must add the somewhat less precise enrollment effects on the number of librarians. To obtain these, the librarian can turn to the data reported in table 2.5.

To make this discussion more specific, let us use some num-bers (selected for arithmetic simplicity rather than realism). Suppose our illustrative librarian works at a private college with 2,500-4,999 students. This librarian would then utilize table A.6, which applies to his category of institution. Sup-pose that in 1971-72 he finds that his library holds 200,000 volumes and that educational expenditures per student at his college are $2,000. Using table 1.4, he will see that in small libraries, the number of volumes held can be expected to grow by 5.4 percent while expenditures per student grow at about 6.1 percent. Hence, for 1972-73, he can project the following figures:

| | |
|---|---|
| Volumes held | 210,800 |
| Expenditures per student | $2,122 |

Now, the table A.6 equation for number of librarians can be written as:

$$\text{Number of librarians} = -0.6153 + 0.3258 \times \text{volumes held}$$
$$+3.9027 \times \text{expenditures per student}$$

with −0.6153 as the constant term. Rounding the coefficients in the equation (for purposes of illustrative simplicity) and inserting the projections just obtained,[6] we have:

$$\text{Number of librarians} = -0.6 + 0.3 \, (21.08)$$
$$+4.0 \, (2.122) \cong 14.$$

This equation gives the librarian his initial projection for the number of professional librarians, indicating as a norm what can be expected to hold for institutions in circumstances similar to those at his.

A major concern of many libraries is the preparation and projection of their overall operating budgets. This task can be accomplished with the aid of equation 5 (i.e., the entries in the fifth column) in the appropriate table from among A.5 to A.12.

The application of this model requires estimates of the level of holdings, acquisitions, and the number of librarians in the year for which the projection is to be made. The sum of these, each multiplied by its associated coefficient in equation 5, plus the constant of the equation, provides an estimate of the required operating budget of the library.

Again, an illustrative calculation may be helpful. Let us assume that a public institution with an enrollment between

6. Note that table A.6 measures number of volumes held in units of 10,000, so that our projected number of volumes becomes 21.08. Similarly, educational expenditures per student are expressed in units of $1,000.

10,000 and 20,000 is preparing its annual budget. Assume that in the forecast year, the collection is expected to hold 1,500,000 volumes; acquisitions are projected at 100,000; and a staff of 50 professional librarians will be employed. (These projections can be obtained in various ways, the simplest being an extrapolation based on tables 1.3 and 1.4.)

The equation for this operating budget (from table A.12) can be written as:

Operating budget = 0.5571 + 0.0139 × volumes held
·+ 0.8139 × volumes added + 0.1317
× professional librarians

where 0.5571 is the constant term. Rounding the coefficients for illustrative simplicity and substituting the projections into the equation in units of 10,000 volumes, we obtain:

Operating budget = 0.56 + 0.014 (150)
+ 0.814 (10) + 0.132 (50) = 17.4.

Since costs are expressed in units of $100,000, the projected budget is $1,740,000.

Two points are noteworthy. A projection of the operating budget can also be carried out with the use of a more aggregate model, whose central equation is estimated for all public institutions (table 2.3). In the illustration just carried out, this calculation calls for a slightly higher budget, totaling $1,839,000. Thus, in each case, there are at least two equations on which a projection can be based: the one based on data for all enrollment sizes simultaneously (table 2.2 or 2.3) and the one fitted to the individual enrollment class data (from tables A.5 to A.12). The precise conditions under which the use of one or the other equation is preferable is a matter of judgment. There is a case for the employment of the equation which has the higher $\bar{R}^2$ if these figures differ markedly for the two equations, but this is not a cast-iron precept.

We might also reiterate here that in the last illustration, the projection provides for an allowance based on collection size

($210,000 in our example) apart from allowances for staff and acquisitions. The only adjustment that remains is one for inflationary effects. Inflation primarily affects the prices of acquisitions and levels of staff salaries. As demonstrated in table 1.4 by the differences between growth rates for book expenditures and volumes added, and between growth rates for salaries and total staff, the price of acquisitions grew at a rate of 4.8 percent per annum (compounded) and staff salaries at 4.4 percent. The expected inflationary impact will be a weighted average of these figures (4.5 percent in our example), the weights being proportional to the share of the budget going to each activity in the most recent period.

The budget can now be converted from our 1968 base to the desired year, say 1973. A price increase of 4.5 percent compounded over five years adds up to a 24.6 percent increase, and the budget is $1,740,000 × 1.246 = $2,168,040.

The type of calculation described in the preceding sections is not meant to deny that at each individual institution there will be additional factors which must be considered in budget preparation. Nor does our calculation pretend to serve as some sort of indicator of optimality. A budget based on the computations described would reflect practices at other institutions comparable to that of the library in question. Our findings do not preclude the possibility that prevailing practices can be improved upon to reduce the costs of a given volume of activity or to improve the service made possible by a given outlay.

However, there is an important reason why budget preparation must take cognizance of prevailing standards in other libraries, as the calculations of this chapter have done. Every college and university must keep up with the standards offered by others if it is to obtain students and faculty members of comparable quality. This element has been critical in the budgeting of faculty salaries and their improvement over the past decade and can certainly play an important role in effective financial planning for libraries.

# Cost Trends and Longer-Range Plans | 3

The literature of library technology has made much of the prospects of an electronic revolution. Extravagant claims and overly sanguine predictions have undoubtedly reduced the credibility of much that has been said about such innovations. Certainly, there is reason to believe that for the immediate future changes in library technology will continue to be gradual. To date, the majority of successful data processing applications in libraries have involved mechanization of nonprofessional tasks such as circulation control and typing of bibliographic aids. At the same time, there are trends in process which may in the next two decades change the range of innovation that is economically feasible.[1] These are: (1) the achievement of a standard format for bibliographic records in machine-readable form and the associated production at the Library of Congress and elsewhere of a sizable data base of such records; (2) a continuing sharp decrease in the cost of certain components of electronic data processing systems; (3) continuing increases in the capacity and reliability of electronic communications channels with concomitant decreases in the unit costs of the channels; and (4) the creation of evolving modular, computer-based library systems, which take advantage of the three other changes just

1. We are particularly grateful to Carl M. Spaulding of the Council on Library Resources for his invaluable contributions to the preparation of this chapter.

41

mentioned. In these systems the electronic computers involved are not a substitute for the intellectual work of professional library personnel. Instead, they facilitate that work and multiply its effect through a great reduction of needless duplication. In addition, they accomplish enormous amounts of nonintellectual work in the form of computer printing of catalog cards, spine labels, order forms, and the like. But because of the growing complexity of the demands upon the librarian and the increase in the quantity of materials to be handled, no decline in the demand for the services of the skilled professional is imminent. In addition, there is every reason to expect that new (and, it is hoped, better) services to library patrons will require large numbers of librarians educated in new library functions, including the application of electronic information-handling systems. In short, library technology is apparently entering a period of important change, but the change will evolve over a period of quite a few years and while unit costs of some functions may gradually begin to level off or even decrease, overall costs of libraries will be appreciably higher than at present.

The cost-trend information gathered in this report suggests that in a few decades some profound modification in the manner in which libraries are run may virtually be inevitable. If this is so (and this chapter will discuss the basis for that assertion), libraries must begin planning for the changeover in a systematic manner, rather than leave the shape of the new arrangement to haphazard developments.

Planning in this area must be undertaken early because of the long lags inherent in the decision process and the very long-term commitment implicit in these decisions. For example, a library building is usually constructed with the expectation that it will serve its users for many decades. A building designed to be compatible only with methods of operation prevalent at the time of its construction may lock the institution into obsolete activity patterns which will constitute an intolerable drain upon its budget. Add to this problem the time lag inherent in the very process of design, and the plea for early planning of future library operations becomes more than a routine reaffirmation of belief in foresight, research, and motherhood!

### Relevance of the Cost Trends

Obviously, economic forces are only one factor among the set of elements that determines the course of developments in library organization. Yet under some circumstances, their role becomes crucial. If the cost of some activity or mode of operation is prohibitive, this fact alone can obviously be decisive. In the process we are now discussing, cost may play this role twice—initially, by limiting severely the libraries' use of electronic equipment, and later, perhaps, by forcing them to embrace it.

Decision making in this area must then take into account future as well as present costs; i.e., it must give heavy weight to the relevant cost trends. Some of these trends have already been reported here. We will presently examine more closely those that are critical for our discussion and also bring out some figures on cost trends in other areas relevant to our topic.

Forecasting on the basis of past trends can often be hazardous. The fact that a statistical series has moved in a particular direction in the past gives us little reason to trust that it will continue on this same course indefinitely. We know too many cases in which very protracted cycles or simply sharp breaks in behavior have led to total departure from linear trends that had been followed for substantial periods. However, as will be shown later, in the case we will be discussing, we have strong analytical reasons for confidence in the belief that the observed trends are likely to continue unchanged at least in direction, if not in absolute magnitude. In other words, in projecting the cost figures which are the basis for our discussion, we are not simply engaging in mechanical extrapolation; we do have a solid analytical basis for our forecast.

In the next section we will examine some of the statistical evidence on comparative cost trends. Then we will digress briefly to review the analytic explanation for these trends, showing the grounds for our belief in their reliability as portents of the future. Finally, we will examine in some detail the nature of their longer-run implications for library operations.

## Some Postwar Trends in Library and Computer Costs

For reasons that will emerge presently, libraries and computers may be considered two opposite polar cases among information channels from the point of view of past and prospective cost behavior. In this section, some data are provided to illustrate the nature of these differences in cost behavior.

As we have already noted, the cost *per unit* of library services has been rising rapidly and steadily *relative to the average cost of commodities* in the United States as a whole while the real cost (cost corrected for changes in purchasing power) of electronic computers has been behaving in precisely the opposite fashion. In brief, library costs have been *rising* sharply while the costs of electronic computers have been *falling*.

Before some illustrative statistics are presented, the interpretation of rising library cost figures merits a bit of discussion. Two obvious—and frequently encountered—explanations of the rising costs of library services are inflation in the general economy and increases in the size of the population served, notably in the size of the student body at colleges and universities. The results summarized here show that neither is a tenable explanation for the bulk of the cost increases. Since the trends are apparent in terms of unit costs (cost per volume held or cost per student), the rises cannot be explained simply as a matter of a larger volume of activity. Of course, if costs per student increase and simultaneously the number of students grows, we can expect a still larger rise in the total budget; but something besides the expansion of the student population underlies the observed trends.

General inflation is not the sole influence underlying the rises, nor can inflation *plus* rising activity levels account for the observed facts. During the postwar period, the price level in the United States was relatively stable until the acceleration of military activities in Vietnam. Our data show that library costs *per unit* have risen at a compound rate far greater than that of the general price level. Obviously, in a period in which the wholesale price index was increasing at an annual rate of less than 1 percent while library costs *per student* increased at more than 5 percent a year compounded, the growth in student body and the rise in price level still leave unexplained an annual rise of more than 4 percent.[2]

We turn now to the data. Figure 3.1 shows how college and university library costs per unit have risen relative to the wholesale price index. In the graph, for comparability, the curves have been put on an index basis (1951 = 100). They show dramatically how much more rapid has been the increase in per unit library costs than that in general price level.

Table 3.1 indicates explicitly these relative growth rates from 1951 to 1969. We see for example that, calculated on a per volume basis, the cost per student of operation of university libraries went up at an annual rate of slightly over 6 percent while during the same period, the wholesale price index was increasing at a rate of less than 1 percent per

2. We do not intend to imply that rising prices have been no problem for libraries. On the contrary, as table 3.1 indicates, prices of books and periodicals, a principal expenditure of libraries, have themselves risen at a rate far exceeding that of the general price level. The point is that in *both* of these activity sectors, there are special economic relationships at work (other than the general economic pressures besetting the economy) which account for their atypical price behavior.

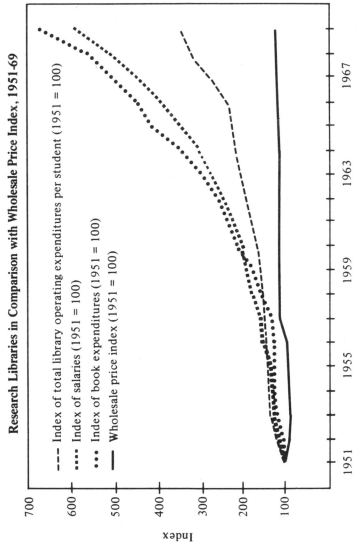

**Figure 3.1**

Unit Costs in Fifty-eight University

Research Libraries in Comparison with Wholesale Price Index, 1951-69

--- Index of total library operating expenditures per student (1951 = 100)

····· Index of salaries (1951 = 100)

•••• Index of book expenditures (1951 = 100)

—— Wholesale price index (1951 = 100)

*Source:* Table 2.2.

46

annum. The table does, indeed, confirm that costs per unit of library services have tended to rise far more rapidly than the price level.

**Table 3.1**

**Growth Rates in per Unit Operating Costs and Prices for Fifty-eight University Research Libraries, Fiscal 1951-69**

| | *Growth Rate per Volume Owned* | *Growth Rate per Student Enrolled* | *Growth Rate in Selected Price Indices* |
|---|---|---|---|
| Total expenditures .......... | 6.3 | 6.1 | — |
| Staff salaries .............. | 5.5 | 5.3 | — |
| Growth rate in wholesale price index (1951-69) ...... | — | — | 0.9 |
| Growth rate in price of library acquisitions (1958-68)............... | — | — | 6.5 |

*Sources:* For library expenditures and staff salaries, Association of Research Libraries (see table 1.3); for growth of wholesale price index, figure 3.2; for growth of library acquisitions, chapter 1.

*Note:* The growth rates have been calculated by logarithmic least squares regression.

Let us contrast this cost behavior with the cost pattern for electronic computer systems. Improvement in the cost-performance ratio for certain principal computer components in the past twenty years has been rather phenomenal. Figure 3.2 illustrates, in a most dramatic way, the decrease in the cost of performing a set of operations, each occurring with a relative frequency corresponding to average commercial use.[3] (In this diagram, a logarithmic scale has been employed to compress the data and reduce the slope of the graph in order

3. The costs of commercial rather than scientific calculations are reported because of their similarity to library operations in the use of storage, comparison, etc. Nevertheless, one must be careful *not* to interpret the reported trends in computation costs to represent the costs of automation in libraries, where the nature of the appropriate equipment may have to be far more specialized and where manual operations will unavoidably continue to play an important role.

# Figure 3.2
## Comparison of Cost of Computation with Wholesale Price Index

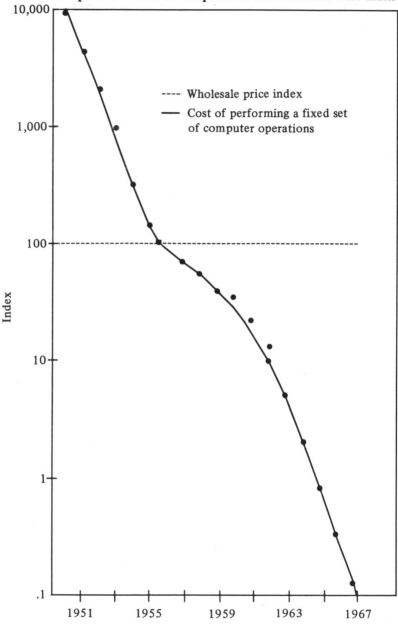

*See notes on facing page.*

to fit it into a standard page.)[4] The cost decrease follows a step-like pattern with the rate of decrease about 55 percent a year (except between 1955 and 1960 when the decrease was about 20 percent).[5]

The cost of on-line storage (computer memory) is perhaps of slightly more direct interest for a comparison with library systems. The reduction in computer storage costs has not been as impressive as the increase in computer performance, but it has nevertheless been quite spectacular. For example, in the 1960s, the speed of ferrite core memories improved by a factor of 4 while the cost per unit decreased by a factor of 7.[6]

Central processing units (CPUs) for computers are expected to experience cost decreases of from 80 to 90 percent by 1980 with large processors showing the greatest percentage reduction. Random-access mass storage devices (e.g., disk files) are likely to exhibit even greater cost decreases during the eighties, reaching a cost per basic unit of storage equal to

---

4. A logarithmic scale is one in which equal intervals represent constant *percentage* increases rather than constant *absolute* increases. For example, if on the vertical scale the first inch above the axis represents an increase in cost from $100 to $200, the second inch will go from $200 to $400, and the third from $400 to $800. That is, the intervals proceed in the geometric sequence 1, 2, 4, 8, 16, etc., rather than the usual arithmetic sequence, 1, 2, 3, etc.

5. The years 1955 to 1966 are reported to have been periods of saturation in the use of old models, and in the years after 1960, there was a sharp increase in the marketing of larger computers.

6. R. J. Petschauer, "Trends in Memory Element and Subsystem Design in the 1970's," *Computer* 3, no. 6 (November-December 1970): 13.

*Sources:* Data from 1950 to 1962, Kenneth E. Knight, "Change in Computer Performance," *Datamation* 12, no. 9 (September 1966): 40-42+. Data from 1963 to 1966, Kenneth E. Knight, "Evolving Computer Performance, 1963-1967," *Datamation* 14, no. 1 (January 1968): 31-35.

*Note:* Each point represents the cost of performing the same "mix" of operations using the computers available during the time period under consideration. The operations used in this mix were grouped into five categories:
1. Fixed add (and subtract) and compare instructions performed
2. Floating add (and subtract) instructions required
3. Multiply instructions
4. Divide instructions
5. Other manipulations and logic instructions

The relative frequencies with which the five operations were used correspond to a typical pattern of commercial use. The year 1956 has been taken as the base year.

no more than 1 percent of today's cost.[7] Generally, this savings will be reflected in the availability of devices with much larger capacities for the current price rather than a 99 percent price reduction for today's devices.

Concurrently, telecommunications technology will continue for some time to provide ever higher capacity methods as well as facilities for transmitting and switching data streams from computer to computer and between user terminals and computers. For the past 130 years, communications technology has advanced with remarkable consistency in that it has, over each successive period of approximately 17 years, provided a new or improved technique having a per channel capacity ten times that of its predecessor. It is entirely possible that this remarkably consistent performance will be improved on in the next two decades.[8]

These items, central processing units, random-access storage, core memory, and telecommunications facilities, are all important elements in library automation systems. Central processing units are the unifying and controlling components of any computer hardware configuration, and the size and speed of the associated core memories directly affect the efficiency of software. Large capacity, low unit-cost random-access storage is vital for the enormous bibliographic data bases which are fundamental for computerization of library functions. Finally, network development and other resource- and facility-sharing operations among libraries cannot be truly efficient until electronic communications channels become highly reliable, relatively low in cost, automatically switched, and capable of carrying very large volumes of digital traffic.

The difference between the rate of change in the general price level and the rates of change of library and computer

7. Frederic G. Withington, "The Next (and Last?) Generation," *Datamation* 18, no. 5 (May 1972): 71-74.

8. James Martin, *Future Developments in Telecommunication* (Englewood Cliffs, N.J.: Prentice-Hall, 1971), p. 341 ff.

costs are small numbers when stated as annual percentages but are not minor matters when compounded for a period of a few years. For example, with a 7 percent rate of increase a variable doubles in a single decade and expands by a factor of 8 in only thirty years (the time interval since the beginning of the second World War).

Specifically, a service now provided by conventional library methods at substantially less than it would cost if provided by means of a computer-based system could become cheaper to do by computer in a few years. At the same time, these overall trends do *not* indicate that a continuing increase in the cost of library operations and a continuing decrease in the cost of computer technology will *necessarily* cause any particular library operation to become less expensive through automation. The susceptibility of the specific function to replacement of human effort by machinery and the way in which the total library operation is organized must be considered. Some human capabilities are very difficult—perhaps impossible—to duplicate or supersede by electronic and mechanical hardware.

More important than the evolving capability of electronic machinery to carry out (or assist with) the tasks presently making up library operations is the potential for using new technological developments and management methods in order to: (1) provide new or improved services to library patrons, (2) enhance greatly the management of resources, and (3) restructure the way libraries and related organizations function individually and collectively. For example, multi-library sharing of infrequently used resources might be facilitated by a computer-based system for more effective determination of the location and availability of those resources. The same system could be used to help select titles appropriate for shared collections and to determine the cost of library resources, services, and facilities required to support curriculum changes being considered in conjunction with resource sharing. In sum, the computer properly applied is but an element, albeit an important one, in a gradual prospective reorganization of the operation of libraries and other information transfer agencies. Consequently, costs in the computer era will be more a function of those new systems whose development is feasible financially than of the costs of computerization of the functions of existing systems. In any event, the overriding constraint will be the funds available.

## A Model of Service and Nonservice Cost Trends

Let us now attempt to account for the behavior of the data just reported.[9] Again, it is convenient to think in terms of two polar cases because they simplify the discussion and do not undermine the validity of the analysis. However, in actuality the economy is composed largely of activities that fall in between the two extremes and share some of the characteristics of each in varying degrees.

We consider two economic activities. In one activity, the quality of the end product is directly dependent on the amount of labor expended per unit of production; as a consequence, it is difficult for technological progress to effect any significant decreases in the quantity of labor input. In the other activity, however, cumulative savings in the labor input occur steadily.

Examples of both types of activity can be easily provided. Among relatively inflexible labor-content activities, one can list education, medicine, live artistic performances, legal services, fire protection, and certain library services. Examples of industries that have benefited over the years from labor-saving innovations are even more numerous: telecommunications, electric power, automotive production, and electronics, to name a few. The examples show that the distinction is a very real one. Moreover, while from time to time, breakthroughs have increased productivity in some activities of the

9. This section is intended as a brief summary of the analysis of Part III, "On the Economics of Library Operations" in Douglas M. Knight and E. Shepley Nourse, *Libraries at Large: Tradition, Innovation, and the National Interest* (New York: R. R. Bowker Co., 1969).

first category, these advances have rarely been followed by a steady stream of labor-saving innovations as has typically been the case in manufacturing. This result has not been a matter of accident. The difference is inherent in the nature of the two types of products and the technology of their supply. The first category consists largely of services requiring personal attention, in which the quality of the end product depends primarily on the amount of human effort devoted to it. Such products are not easily standardized or automated. In many cases, the quantity of labor involved per unit of output is virtually fixed by the nature of the product; e.g., a performance of a trio scored for one-half hour clearly requires a one and a half man-hour performance.

Now, the evidence indicates that wages in the labor-inflexible industries have often lagged behind those in the rest of the economy, but have generally caught up over longer periods. For example, while right after the war school teachers' wages had fallen behind those in industry, the gap has now been closed. Economic pressures simply do not permit growing divergences in real wages in different economic activities, for, if growing disparities were to persist, labor would move into the increasingly better paid occupations, and the resulting shortages would force wages up in the activities where they had lagged. A good deal of evidence shows that things do work out this way in practice.

The implication of the analysis for the cost behavior of the service and manufacturing sectors is straightforward. With costs of labor rising at comparable rates, but labor requirements falling cumulatively and steadily in the one sector while remaining fairly constant in the other, a differential in cost behavior becomes inevitable. Costs of the service sector must rise steadily and cumulatively relative to those in the remainder of the economy at a percentage rate directly related to the differential in their productivity.

If wages in the economy rise at a rate of 5 percent per year, and productivity in manufacturing increases by 4 percent per annum while productivity in the services remains almost unchanged, costs of manufactured goods will go up at an annual rate of 1 percent, but those of services will rise at 5 percent. The difference in the technologies of the two sectors forces this differential upon them, and, with occasional exceptions, we can expect such a differential to persist year after year.

The empirical evidence supports this conclusion. In one personal service after another, costs per unit of output have risen over 4 percent more rapidly over the postwar period than the rate of increase in price level. The *relative* costs *per unit* of these services have doubled every fourteen years and quadrupled over less than three decades. Understandably these sectors have faced budgetary difficulties that have grown more critical with the passage of time.

As we have already noted, conventional library operation is a fairly inflexible labor-content activity; its success requires personal services and depends heavily on the amount of human thought and attention devoted to it. The preceding analysis can thus help explain a significant portion of the rising demands upon library budgets.

### Other Sources of Rising Library Costs

Like any analytic model, the preceding analysis constitutes something of an oversimplification of the facts. Library cost increases over the postwar period obviously reflect to some extent the general expansion in the nation's institutions of higher education, including the proliferation of new programs. Yet the fact that, calculated on a *per student* basis, library expenditures increased at some 6 percent per year suggests that there is more to the matter than the expansion of higher education.

The volume of world book production also has been increasing very rapidly, implying that a library must acquire more books per year simply to obtain the same percentage of new publications for its collections. Added to this increase in production is the rising price of books and journals. As indicated in table 3.1, their price on the average has increased at just about the same annual rate as library expenditures per enrolled student—at something in excess of 6 percent per year.

Each of these elements must be assigned some role in any adequate explanation of the rising costs of library operations. Yet over the long run, a critical place must be assigned to the technological component stressed in the preceding section. Unlike the service character of library operations, many of the influences that have just been listed may well be transitory. Thus, for example, the expansion in educational programs as well as in the size of student bodies is undoubtedly decelerating.

Moreover, some of these cost-increasing influences themselves are engendered by the cost problem imposed by service technology, this difficulty thereby affecting the libraries indirectly as well as directly. For example, the scope for productivity increases in the publications industry has apparently proven very limited, and our analysis therefore also helps to explain the rise in costs of books and periodicals, which has contributed so much to the growth in library expenses.

Finally, we should observe that other service industries have exhibited cost patterns very similar to those characterizing the libraries. For example, between 1949 and 1969, the cost per pupil-day of elementary education in the United States rose some 6.5 percent per year. At public and private universities, over the two decades, instructional costs per student rose at average rates of 5.0 and 7.5 percent per year, respectively. Between 1946 and 1965, hospital expenses per patient-day, after elimination of the effects of the increase in personnel per patient, grew at an annual rate of 6.2 percent.[10] The similarity in all these figures certainly lends credence to the notion that some common element is at work.

10. These figures, some of them updated and revised, are based on D. A. Bradford, R. A. Malt, and W. E. Oates, "The Rising Cost of Local Public Services: Some Evidence and Reflections," *National Tax Journal* 22, no. 2 (June 1969): 185-202.

## Implications of the Analysis

The simple model of service and manufacturing cost trends presented earlier in this chapter should be of interest for a number of reasons. The analysis shows that the rising costs of library operations emanate from what may be described as the technological structure of library operations. The most frequently cited villains—inefficiency and mismanagement—need have nothing to do with the problem, and general inflation explains only a limited part of it. Similar cost trends have been documented for various activities in other inflexible labor-content portions of the economy. The largest single activity of American municipalities in terms of size of budgetary requirements is education, and we have just seen that educational costs per pupil rise at just about the same rate as those of library services. The same is true of various other public services. For nonprofit institutions such as hospitals, private universities, and orchestras, costs have been rising about as rapidly. Among business enterprises in the services sector, one finds automotive insurance, restaurants, and law firms, and here again the trend is similar. The diversity of areas whose cost trends are consistent with the predictions of the model is important as is the fact that the differences in cost trends between service and nonservice activities continue through all sorts of economic circumstances—periods of inflation and recession. These trends indicate, in accord with the analysis, that this cost increase for services is not a fortuitous phenomenon whose effects can be expected to be transitory nor one ascribable to peculiar circumstances within one or a few activities.

Another important implication of our analysis is that the source of the rising relative costs of library operations—its *comparatively* slow rate of labor-saving innovation—means that society can, if it chooses, meet these rising costs. The rapid growth of productivity in other sectors in the economy that drives up the costs of service activities automatically increases the wealth of the community. The notion that a community can afford less in the way of services because the productivity of its manufacturing is increasing is a patent absurdity. While services will undoubtedly continue to grow more expensive, the analysis shows that the community will well be able to afford to pay these rising costs, and that failure to do so may simply represent a misguided reallocation of social priorities rather than an unavoidable economy measure.

Finally, the analysis suggests that certain components of electronic data processing systems do not suffer from the technological cost problems that now beset libraries. Electronics has benefited more than most industries from increased productivity through innovation. Few areas have proven to provide such fertile ground for technological change. The implications of our model are perfectly consistent with the cost behavior of these two activities as indicated earlier by our statistics.

The model leads us to conclude that the observed cost patterns are neither fortuitous nor temporary. The same technological differences that have accounted for the divergent cost trends for data processing systems and conventional library operations in the past are likely to be with us in the years to come. This stability is precisely why cost forecasting in this area is a reasonable undertaking and why one can have some degree of confidence in its results. For the analysis offers us an explanation of the behavior of relative costs that indicates why the future can be expected to bring with it a continuation of the trends observed in the past for the two types of activities, trends whose differences are substantial and significant.

### Longer-Run Implications for Library Operations

There are no doubt many reasons why the use of electronic systems in libraries has proceeded far less rapidly than some of its more sanguine advocates had predicted. In part, the electronic systems seem to have proven less flexible and less useful (at least in their present state of design) than had been claimed. In addition, library operations are more complex than computer adherents had realized. Undoubtedly also, as in any profession, there is some degree of natural conservatism and resistance to innovation.

Yet, a major impediment to a change in library operations turned out to be the cost of the electronic equipment itself and of its operation. The investment in purchase or rental of the equipment is enormous, and rapid obsolescence does not make matters easier. Moreover, sophisticated equipment requires the use of highly skilled personnel for maintenance, operation, programming, and so on, and such personnel are never cheap. As a result, the use of electronic equipment for the performance of library functions has been, for the most part, financially prohibitive.

However, the long-run trends—if they continue to behave as in the recent past—are likely to change the cost relationship dramatically and may conceivably do so more quickly than is generally expected. With recent rates of change in their costs continuing, only a decade would be required to eliminate a ten-fold operational cost differential between service activity and a purely electronic substitute (assuming a purely electronic substitute exists or can be developed). By the time two decades had passed, the cost of the labor-intensive conventional process would have risen to twenty times that of its electronic substitute!

Such an extrapolation undoubtedly exaggerates matters. It is quite possible that the burst of innovation that has accompanied the inauguration of computer technology may not continue very long. In any event, the electronic processing cost calculations as they have been derived here are not directly applicable to libraries. The requirements of library computerization are quite unique, and the necessary technology is still far from being settled. It would be foolish to take data derived from the application of general-purpose computers for other uses and simply attempt to use them unmodified and unanalyzed as a predictor of future library costs.

Yet the figures are suggestive. They indicate that within the foreseeable future, electronization of a significant portion of library operations may perhaps become feasible financially, and in some cases may become unavoidable. For, with a time path of costs such as the libraries have experienced, not much time is required before the use of some conventional methods is priced out of consideration. Obviously, the date at which this circumstance occurs will vary by library and by the operation in question. Some critical parts of the workings of the library will probably never lend themselves to electronic assistance to any significant extent. The point of this discussion is not to argue that the computer can, or will, or should do everything, but merely to indicate that in those aspects of library operation for which the computer is potentially useful, the cost trends will ultimately render its use feasible financially.

Computerization and electronic operation are not the only alternatives to conventional library operations. For example, proposals for increased sharing of resources among libraries may prove a promising means to decelerate the expansion in the size of individual collections. Microfilm, microfiche, and other types of miniaturization may help reduce growing storage costs, as will be emphasized in the next section. Both these alternatives can be expected to depend upon, and be imbedded in, electronic technology and each other. At present, resource sharing is commonly inefficient and has a high per unit cost. It appears highly likely that message communication, record keeping, and document transmission for resource sharing will, in the coming years, be more and more efficiently carried out with the aid of advanced telecommunications under computer direction. An increasing amount of resource sharing may also be effected by computer-controlled retrieval, inexpensive duplication, and rapid delivery of microforms. A more advanced system would transmit images of the computer-retrieved microforms by telefacsimile.

Emphasis must be given to the fact that while hardware and software for these systems are technically feasible even now, their utilization in practice on any substantial scale would almost certainly take a decade or more and would require hard-won progress in nontechnological areas. For example, legislative and judicial action would have to be taken on copyright matters, user-acceptance of microforms would need to be improved, and new methods of remunerating publishers would have to be worked out.

The authors of this volume lay no claim to expertise in the technology of library operation, and there is nothing further from our objective than specific recommendations about the type of innovation that will prove most amenable to use by libraries. Rather, our intention is merely to point out the implications of current cost trends and our analytic results, which indicate that these trends can be expected to persist over the foreseeable future. The economist is in no position to judge in any detail how the shape of library operations will change with the passage of time. He can, however, assert with some degree of confidence that some fairly radical changes may become inevitable within a matter of decades.

### Other Relevant Trends

In chapter 1 we examined growth rates of various library indices and came across several that were rather high. One growth rate particularly pertinent for this discussion is the figure for volumes held, which over the two decades investigated grew at a cumulative rate of more than 4 percent per annum. At that rate, the average size of a library collection doubles in less than eighteen years and quadruples in less than thirty-five years.

The storage problems that this prospect entails are clear enough. But the volumes held statistics may well understate the problem by a considerable margin. For the evidence indicates that the expansion of libraries is in fact accelerating, and at a remarkable rate. The number of volumes *added* has been increasing far more rapidly than the number of volumes held. The former has been growing cumulatively at an average annual rate exceeding 7 percent. Within four decades, if this trend continues, the number of volumes added annually will be sixteen times as large as it is today. The processing and storage problems may prove overwhelming for a very substantial proportion of college and university libraries.

Well before that time one may expect the search for alternative forms of storage and retrieval to become a matter of the highest priority. Already it has begun to emerge as a critical issue, and various new forms of microfilm are now available. However, most of these forms have serious drawbacks, such as the requirement for special equipment which the reader must utilize at a location away from his normal working and reading area, or high cost when produced in small numbers of copies. Here again, it has been suggested that electronic means can be found to help matters, but specific and detailed remedial methods have, at least as yet, not been designed.

### Requisites of Planning

In these circumstances, an institution with a large conventional library plant that does not lend itself to conversion may be at an enormous disadvantage. To protect their interests, institutions should begin as soon as possible to examine the implications of library cost trends for their own operations and to lay out procedures for an orderly transition that keeps down dislocations and costs.

Most of the work of library planning, of course, requires skills and knowledge which the economist normally does not possess. Such planning calls for intimate acquaintance with both the details of library operations and the capabilities—current and prospective—of the pertinent types of electronic equipment.

Yet, three observations are perhaps useful for us to offer:

1. Continuing surveillance of the cost trends of library operations, with particular attention to significant changes in any of these trends, is desirable.

2. In designing additions to library plants, serious consideration should be given to the incorporation into the design of elements of *flexibility* which permit easier conversion from conventional to electronic models of operation. However, flexibility is itself *not* a free commodity, and a balance between cost and flexibility must be sought for each library. A building readily convertible from one type of operation to another will be more expensive than one much more specialized. Moreover, large-scale conversion to electronic modes of operation or a fundamental redefinition of the functions of libraries is impractical for the immediate future. But since the costs of conventional operations are likely to continue to rise so dramatically, built-in flexibility, despite its cost, may prove to be the most rational approach to the matter. In any event, this possibility should be investigated carefully with some study of the nature of the specific design modifications required, the likely range of their costs, and their relative suitability for libraries that differ in size and in other characteristics.

3. Because ultimate responsibility for the proper design and performance of new library systems lies with the professional library staff, the movement of schools of library science into study areas dealing with library management, computer technology, systems analysis, and the economics of library operations is highly desirable. While not turning librarians into experts in these areas, such programs do enable them to work with the specialists, thereby facilitating the rapid and optimal employment of the newer management methods.

## Concluding Comment

The analysis of cost trends just described shows that the observed behavior of costs of library operations and of related activities cannot be considered a chance occurrence. The trends arise at least in considerable part out of the nature of the technology involved and hence they can be expected, with a considerable degree of confidence, to continue for the foreseeable future.

These cost changes are likely to have a revolutionary impact on the nature of library operations, and the general outlines of these changes can be anticipated. Increased sophistication in technology and recourse to automated equipment may be unavoidable within a matter of decades. So profound a change can be extremely disturbing to the orderly functioning of libraries unless steps are taken early to plan for the transition and to assure that its advent occurs in an organized manner.

# 4 | The Data

The scope and reliability of an empirical study are determined in large measure by the quality and extent of coverage of the available data. Although information shortages can at times by remedied by collection of primary data, such an undertaking is, in practice, very expensive and time-consuming. For this reason, every attempt was made in this study to work with data already gathered by other organizations. Two major data compilations, not previously subjected to searching analysis, were used as the basis of this study. These are: (1) data gathered by the U.S. Office of Education, National Center for Educational Statistics, for *Library Statistics of Colleges and Universities: Data for Individual Institutions, Fall 1967* and *Fall 1968* (Washington, D.C.: Government Printing Office, 1969) and (2) selected data items on fifty-eight university research libraries which are members of the Association of Research Libraries (the data are on an IBM card deck and have been kindly provided to us by the University Libraries and Audio Visual Center, Purdue University, Lafayette, Indiana).[1]

In the following sections, we describe the scope of these data and their suitability for the study and explain their complementary character. The chapter will be concluded with a number of suggestions on how the available data base might be supplemented to facilitate future research.

1. We are grateful to William S. Dix for first calling this source to our attention.

## Library Statistics of Colleges and Universities

The information provided in *Library Statistics of Colleges and Universities* (which we shall refer to as *Library Statistics*) includes data for over 2,000 college libraries for 1967 and 1968. Virtually the entire range of colleges and universities is covered, from two-year institutions to universities. Staff members of the Office of Education have been most helpful in providing us with the computer tapes on which these data are stored.

A primary attraction of *Library Statistics,* in addition to its extremely wide coverage, is the wealth of data it contains. Indeed, *Library Statistics* may well represent the most comprehensive data source on university libraries available at this time. To convey the extent of its coverage, a listing of all variables for which *Library Statistics* gives data is provided in table 4.1. These variables include library personnel, their salaries, other categories of expenditure, detailed acquisitions data, and information characterizing the size of the collection and its mix.

As is often the case with tapes containing basic data, the form in which the data were recorded on the *Library Statistics* tapes did not permit us to use it directly in our statistical analysis. A new program to extract the variables and place them in a new file had to be designed.

## Association of Research Libraries Data

The main advantage of the information provided by the Association of Research Libraries (ARL) is the length of the period (nineteen years) for which data for an identical group of institutions are provided; in this respect, the ARL information is a perfect complement to the figures provided in *Library Statistics.* Thus, in dealing with questions for which the time dimension is most important—the determination of the magnitude of inflationary effects on library costs, for example—we relied on the ARL-Purdue data. On the other hand, questions relating to the determinants of operating costs could best be handled with the aid of the *Library Statistics* material.

The number of series covered in the ARL data is, however, very limited compared with those found in *Library Statistics.*

### Table 4.1

### Variables Included in Office of Education
### Library Statistics Data, Fall 1968

Opening fall enrollment
Total enrollment
Undergraduate full-time enrollment
Number of volumes, end of year, 1966-67
Number of volumes added during year
Number of volumes withdrawn during year
Number of volumes, end of year, 1967-68
Number of reels microfilm, end of year
Number of units microtext, end of year
Number of periodical titles, end of year, 1967-68
Number of serial titles, end of year, 1967-68
Interlibrary, number of items borrowed
Interlibrary, nonreturnable items supplied
Interlibrary, returnable items supplied
Salaries, regular library staff, actual, 1967-68
Salaries, regular library staff, budget, 1968-69
Salary equivalent, contributed-services staff, actual, 1967-68
Salary equivalent, contributed-services staff, budget, 1968-69
Wages, students and hourly assistants, actual, 1967-68
Wages, students and hourly assistants, budget, 1968-69
Expenditures, books and library materials, actual, 1967-68
Expenditures, books and library materials, budget, 1968-69
Expenditures for binding, actual, 1967-68
Expenditures for binding, budget, 1968-69
Other operating expenditures, actual, 1967-68
Other operating expenditures, budget, 1968-69
Total expenditures for library, actual, 1967-68
Total expenditures for library, budget, 1968-69
Noncharged services for binding
Automation services
Other services
Number of hours of student assistance during year
Number of hours of other assistance during year
Total educational and general expenses
Educational and general expenditures, budget, 1968-69

Specifically, for each of the fifty-eight libraries, the following statistics are covered: (1) volumes held in the collection; (2) volumes added to the collection; (3) money expended for books, periodicals, and binding; (4) salaries expense; (5) wage expense; (6) professional staff size; (7) nonprofessional staff size; (8) lowest professional salary paid;

**Table 4.1**—*Continued*

Full-time institutional professional staff
Part-time institutional professional staff
Full-time equivalent of part-time professional staff
Number of associate/assistant librarians, full time
Number of associate/assistant librarians, full-time equivalent of part-time
Number of heads of library units, full-time
Number of heads of library units, full-time equivalent of part-time
Number of other professional librarians, full time
Number of other professional librarians, full-time equivalent of part-time
Number of other professional personnel, full time
Number of other professional personnel, full-time equivalent of part-time
Number of nonprofessional personnel, full time
Number of nonprofessional personnel, full-time equivalent of part-time
Number of total library staff, full time
Number of total library staff, full-time equivalent of part-time
Contract salary of chief librarian
Mean salary, associate/assistant librarians, 9 months
Mean salary, heads of major library units, 9 months
Mean salary, other professional librarians, 9 months
Mean salary, other professional staff, 9 months
Mean salary, nonprofessional staff, 9 months
Mean salary, associate/assistant librarians, 12 months
Mean salary, heads of major library units, 12 months
Mean salary, other professional librarians, 12 months
Mean salary, other professional staff, 12 months
Mean salary, nonprofessional staff, 12 months
Number of associate/assistant librarians, 9 months
Number of heads of major library units, 12 months
Number of other professional librarians, 9 months
Number of other professional staff, 9 months
Number of nonprofessional staff, 9 months
Number of associate/assistant librarians, 12 months
Number of heads of major library units, 12 months
Number of other professional librarians, 12 months
Number of other professional staff, 12 months
Number of nonprofessional staff, 12 months

and (9) total expenditures. In addition, for some universities and years, statistics are provided for total reported enrollment, reported graduate student enrollment, and number of Ph.D. degrees granted.

The paucity of general institutional data in this file is particularly unfortunate. For example, statistics on total educational and general expenses of the institution are not included, nor are expenditures on research.

### Suggestions for New Data

There are two primary prerequisites for continuing research on developments and trends in library operations. First, appropriate data must be available, and, of equal importance, the data must be organized in a manner which permits a prompt and inexpensive processing.

The scope of the data currently gathered for the annual publication of *Library Statistics* is very extensive, and only a few additions might be considered.

One important factor which undoubtedly influences the size and mix of the library's book collection and professional staff is the size and type of the graduate program. We found that this information is not provided by the available figures on the FTE (full-time equivalent) enrollment of graduate students. Consideration might be given to the possibility of reporting the number of advanced degrees (M.A.s and Ph.D.s) separately by broad areas.

Another statistic of interest is the number of duplicate volumes in the collection. Such data would enable one to determine the extent to which an increase in collection size, associated with a rise in enrollment, reflects an increase in duplicates. Thought might also be given to the gathering of information on the proportion of foreign language and foreign-published volumes within each collection since these publications may, over the long run, be subject to differing price trends.

The most serious deficiency of the *Library Statistics* survey is not, however, a limited data base, but the difficulties of processing and analyzing a body of data of such dimensions (over 2,000 institutions). Although this problem is mitigated somewhat by the analytical results published by *Library Statistics of Colleges and Universities: Analytic Report, Fall 1968* (U.S. Office of Education), the data as published and as stored on the computer tapes can be processed only at great cost. We would therefore recommend that ways of improving the accessibility and manageability of those data already being gathered be explored. One possibility might be early publication of the data for a sample of institutions, properly stratified by type and size. If such a sample survey can be provided on card decks, or on tapes (which can be used with greater ease), research by many interested organizations would be greatly facilitated.

Since it is reasonable to assume that *Library Statistics* will become the major source of library data, steps may also be taken to achieve greater uniformity between it and the Association of Research Libraries data base, with respect to both the scope and the definitions of the items covered. For example, *Library Statistics* divides a library staff into three categories while the ARL employs only two. Given the easy accessibility of the ARL data, marginal additions to its data base and conformity with *Library Statistics* definitions would prove enormously useful.

# 5 | Summary

## Growth Rates

In our study, we sought to break the analysis down by category of institution, eschewing aggregation as far as the data would permit. This procedure was designed to provide the individual librarian with results that applied closely to the circumstances of his own institution rather than to a hodge-podge of disparate institutions. In our study of time trends, we were able to break our sample of fifty-eight institutions (twenty-three private and thirty-five public) into four size categories defined in terms of volumes held and four growth categories based on percentage rate of increase in the number of volumes held. For each of these, annual percentage rates of increase for each of fifteen variables were calculated for the two decades extending from 1950 through 1969. The variables studied were total enrollment, volumes held, volumes held per student, volumes added, volumes added per student, total personnel, professional staff, professional staff as a percentage of total personnel, nonprofessional staff, total expenditures, expenditures per student, salaries and wages, salaries and wages as a percentage of total expenditures, book expenditures, and book expenditures as a percentage of total expenditures.

In examining our analysis of trends, it should be recognized that they are based on data for two decades during which higher education was relatively untroubled by financial problems. For a variety of reasons, some of them discussed in chapter 3, we are apparently at the end of an era and entering a period of financial stringency, which will inevitably lead to sharp breaks with a number of the financial trends of the recent past. However, the data on past cost trends, in a sense, themselves herald some of these difficulties, for it is hard to imagine indefinite continuation of the rates of growth of expenditure that characterized the postwar period.

The following are some of our most noteworthy results:

1. A number of variables showed remarkably consistent growth patterns throughout the period, suggesting the usefulness of their growth rates for purposes of projection. While most of these variables are themselves only components of total library expenditures, a variable whose own growth rate was fairly constant, each of its elements could not necessarily have been expected to increase at a steady rate. Those variables whose growth patterns were erratic were precisely those for which such behavior could have been anticipated on statistical grounds: they were all ratios (e.g., volumes added divided by number of students) whose statistical behavior is usually unstable for reasons discussed in chapter 1. The variables with highly consistent growth patterns included volumes held, total library expenditures, salaries and wages, and book expenditures. There was also very little intertemporal variability in the growth rates of volumes added, total personnel, professional staff, and nonprofessional staff. Unstable growth patterns characterized volumes held per student, volumes added per student, salaries and wages as a percentage of total expenditures, and book expenditures as a percentage of total expenditures.

2. Over the two decades, the growth rates of a number of the critical variables were remarkably high. They were not particularly high in relation to other college and university costs (over the two-decade period 1949-69, cost of educa-

tion per student in public and private universities grew at average annual rates of 5.0 and 7.5 percent, compounded, respectively). However, in terms of their implications for future library costs, the growth rates of these variables *were* very high. For example, a cost figure growing at 6 percent per year doubles every twelve years, quadruples every twenty-four years, and octuples every thirty-six years, approximately. We list the largest of the growth figures for all libraries combined in table 5.1.

**Table 5.1**

**Annual Percentage Growth Rates
for Selected Library Variables**

| | Annual Percentage Growth Rate |
|---|---|
| Book expenditures . . . . . . . . . . . . . . . . . . . . . . . . . | 11.4 |
| Total library expenditures . . . . . . . . . . . . . . . . . . | 10.5 |
| Salaries and wages . . . . . . . . . . . . . . . . . . . . . . . | 9.7 |
| Volumes added . . . . . . . . . . . . . . . . . . . . . . . . . . . | 6.6 |
| Nonprofessional staff . . . . . . . . . . . . . . . . . . . . . | 6.3 |
| Expenditures per student . . . . . . . . . . . . . . . . . . | 6.1 |

All of these figures represent highly stable growth patterns over the two-decade period studied and all of them exceed 6 percent, some by a considerable margin. These patterns are not totally unchangeable in the future, but they do portend critical financial issues, similar to those that face colleges and universities as a whole.

3. In the smaller university research libraries in our sample, the rates of growth of volumes held and of volumes added have been considerably greater than in the larger libraries. For example, in large libraries, the number of volumes added has grown somewhat less than 6.5 percent per year while in small libraries the figure is 8 percent per annum. By implication, libraries have been moving toward

some reduction in inequality in the size of their collections with the passage of time.

4. Despite substantial growth, the size of collections has hardly kept up with (indeed it may have fallen slightly behind) the magnitude of the student body. This fact helps to confirm the impression that the size of the student body is not the prime determinant of the scale of library operations.

5. Over the period in question, the size of the professional staff has declined relative to the number of nonprofessionals at a rate of about 1.5 percent a year. In part this decline is the result of widespread efforts on the part of library administrators to distinguish between professional and nonprofessional activities and to utilize the services of the professional staff as far as possible entirely for professional work. In addition, staff size has declined in comparison with the number of students served as well as in comparison with the size of collections and acquisitions. This decline undoubtedly represents an economy measure.

6. Over the two decades studied, library expenditures *per student* have risen at a compounded rate of 6.1 percent per annum, as already noted. Since during this period the general price level rose by only some 1.5 percent per year, the rise in library costs is explained neither by the growth in the constituency served nor by general inflation in the economy. Of course, rising book costs and other costs over which libraries have no control have contributed substantially to their financial problems. However, even in periods when the general price level in the United States, as measured by the consumer price index, has been remarkably stable, the costs of library operations, like all costs of higher education, have continued to mount. An explanation of a principal component of this important phenomenon is offered in chapter 3.

The figures calculated in chapter 1 are, of course, usable not only in making the sorts of observations about developments in the nature of library operations that have just been offered but also in projecting future growth and planning budgets. Thus, for example, a librarian in a small research library seeking to construct a budget for the subsequent year should find it highly desirable to know that in comparable institutions the size of the nonprofessional staff has grown very consistently at a compounded rate in the neighborhood of 8.5 percent.

### Analysis of Library Costs

In studying library costs and other such critical elements, our objective was to determine what variables can be taken to determine their magnitudes and to quantify the influence of each of these variables. For example, we found that size of library staff can largely be explained (predicted) in the statistical sense on the basis of just four variables: size of collection, educational expenditures per student, and type and size of institution. To quantify the influence of one of these variables, it was found that if two public institution libraries differ in size by 100,000 volumes, we can expect—all other things being equal—that the library with the larger collection will have 5.5 more professional librarians than the other.

To determine these relationships, the analytic procedures had to be varied in two fundamental respects from the study of growth rates. First, the analysis was based on cross-sectional rather than time series data; that is, it was based on a comparison of data for different institutions, all at the same period of time, rather than a comparison of statistics applying to different points in time for a fixed sample of libraries. Second, we had to employ a multivariate analysis rather than simply compare the behavior of some two variables without taking into account the influence of the others. Thus, in the preceding illustration, a simple correlation between size of professional staff and magnitude of collection would very likely show a highly imperfect association between the two because of the influence of other variables which will disturb their relationship. Only by using a statistical analysis which deals with the more influential variables simultaneously can one hope to disentangle their individual influences. Of course, we were able to utilize only those variables for which statistics are available, and we were forced to leave out of consideration important variables such as the proliferation of new teaching and research programs.

The following are among the results of the multivariate analysis of chapter 2:

1. Private institutions tend to have more professional and nonprofessional staff members (e.g., in institutions with 10,000 or more students, the average nonprofessional staff was 127 in private and 98 in public institutions). However, size of collection and educational expenditures per student seem to account for these differences almost completely. In both private and public institutions, a 100,000-volume difference in size of collection corresponds, *ceteris paribus,* to a ten-person increase in the size of nonprofessional staff. However, on the average, a given increase in educational outlays per student yields an increase in number of librarians in private institutions three times as large as in public institutions. In private institutions the size of staff is also much more closely related to magnitude of enrollment than in public institutions. In both cases, the effect of enrollment on staffing is surprisingly small: in public institutions approximately one librarian is added when the number of students is increased by 1,000.

2. The volume of acquisitions has been shown to be affected by size of collection, educational expenditures per student, and size of enrollment. Larger libraries tend to have substantially larger volumes of acquisitions. Thus, one public institution library holding 10,000 more volumes than another will typically also acquire some 450 more volumes per year than the smaller library. The library size variable played a somewhat smaller role in private colleges

and universities. On the other hand, educational expenditures for the institution as a whole appear to affect acquisitions more in private than in public institutions. A private institution spending $100 more in educational outlays per student than another will typically acquire 125 more volumes per year than the other. As we have pointed out before, there are many local factors that affect these relationships.

3. Levels of library operating costs are explained almost completely (in the statistical sense) by collection size, level of acquisitions, staff, enrollment, and type of institution. We found the following associations: (a) While a difference of 10,000 in the number of volumes held increases library expenses more than $5,000 on the average for private institutions, no such clear relationship exists for public institutions; (b) an addition of one volume corresponds to a $10 increase in costs for both public and private institutions.

The results of this portion of the study are usable directly in library budgeting and planning. However, their mode of utilization is somewhat less obvious than is the manner in which the growth rate data can be employed. Chapter 2 concludes with an explicit discussion of this type of application and with detailed illustrations of the procedures to be employed.

## Library Costs: Longer-Term Trends

Unlike the chapters that precede it, chapter 3 is primarily qualitative in nature. It undertakes to explain in terms of the technology of library operations the reasons for the rapid rise in library costs. This analysis shows that such cost increases are a direct consequence of the association between the amount of human effort employed and the range of library services that can be offered. The analysis is important for several reasons. First, it dispels the notion that inefficiency, any more than inflation or the increase in size of student body, can be blamed for the phenomenon. Rather, our analysis shows that the observed cost trends are very much a matter of the technology of library operations which, so long as one adheres to traditional modes of library operation, is largely beyond the librarian's control. Second, the analysis indicates that these cost trends are no chance phenomenon likely to prove transitory. Finally, the model suggests that in the long run, some fundamental changes in the mode of library operations may become inevitable, though obviously it may prove impossible to change some operations without unacceptable losses in quality.[1]

The remainder of the chapter pursues this last point. In particular, the chapter demonstrates that in recent years the cost of information storage and retrieval by electronic means has exhibited trends precisely the reverse of those of conventional library operations. The electronic processes have been decreasing in cost at a spectacular rate. The long-term implications of these trends are discussed in the chapter, which also considers what librarians can do to plan for an orderly and advantageous adaptation to differential cost trends. These trends may indeed render inevitable some very fundamental changes in the form of library operations, not only through the use of electronic processing (which is likely to be helpful only in some parts of library operations) but also through increased cooperation among libraries, perhaps involving division of fields of responsibility and increased use of new forms of publication such as microfiche. The authors of this report are not qualified to consider and evaluate in any detail the relative merits and range of applicability of

1. While the innovations in prospect are likely to affect the nature of the libraries' ability to respond to user desires, the effects need not always be adverse. For example, while use of uniform classifications by different libraries may inhibit reclassification and reshelving in response to the desires of scholars at individual institutions, electronic methods may make it far easier to prepare bibliographic information.

such innovations. They can merely consider the implications of current cost trends for the likelihood of the utilization of new technologies in some form and combination in the future.

## The Data

Chapter 4 summarizes the characteristics of the data that were utilized for the study in terms of the information they included, their sources, their comparability, and their limitations. The chapter shows that while the Association of Research Libraries data offer information extending over a number of years, the amount of information they provide about individual libraries and the colleges or universities of which they are a part is much more limited than the material offered by the Office of Education.

Finally, a few suggestions are offered for additional data whose collection in the future may be desirable. We proposed that consideration be given to the collection and publication of data on size and composition of graduate programs, and on duplicates in library collections. We suggested further that data be published regularly for a manageable sample of institutions carefully selected and stratified, in order to facilitate their analysis and to assure comparability and maximum usefulness of the data.

## Libraries in Private and Public Institutions

Our statistical analysis has indicated a number of differences in the operations and budgeting of libraries in public and private institutions. Although broad generalizations on the nature of these differences may be misleading because of the great diversity of individual institutions, an outline of our main findings in the area may nevertheless be useful if accepted with considerable reservation.

The policies of private institutions as a group seem to permit them to adapt more fully to differences in circumstances than do those of public institutions. While among public institutions the relationship between the number of librarians and enrollment is weak and relatively haphazard, among private institutions the number of librarians employed increases more nearly proportionately as enrollment rises.

An even more striking observation is the significant positive association between educational expenditures per student (excluding library expenditures) and library services (acquisitions, staff) displayed by private institutions. That such a relationship is not as pronounced in public institutions may suggest a lack of balance between instructional and library programs in these institutions as a group. The picture just drawn must be qualified for the very small private institutions (enrollment 1,000-2,500). The libraries in this group of private colleges appear to be seriously short of staff, and their compensation levels seem substantially lower than those in their public counterparts.

Finally, acquisition costs per volume show differing patterns in public and private institutions. In the latter, per unit cost rises consistently as we move to successively larger enrollment classes while in public institutions, this relationship is hardly apparent. Additional study would be necessary to determine whether these differences are ascribable to budgetary constraints or are a reflection of differences in objectives or institutional arrangements.

# Appendix

## Table A.1

## Mean Values of Various Library Statistics for Private Institutions

| | ENROLLMENT | | | | |
|---|---|---|---|---|---|
| | *1,000-2,499* | *2,500-4,999* | *5,000-9,999* | *10,000-19,999* | *20,000+* |
| Total enrollment, 1967 | 1,482 | 3,214 | 7,077 | 13,382 | 17,268 |
| Volumes held, 1966-67 | 99,690 | 179,290 | 431,180 | 1,018,050 | 1,274,910 |
| Volumes added, 1967-68 | 6,810 | 12,260 | 27,770 | 63,340 | 70,380 |
| Cost of volumes added | 44,000 | 103,900 | 221,700 | 481,900 | 537,400 |
| Total library operating costs | 122,100 | 269,400 | 639,100 | 1,580,300 | 1,827,500 |
| Educational expenditures per student | 1,583 | 1,648 | 2,835 | 4,040 | 3,577 |
| Percentage of collection in physical sciences, biomedicine, technology | 16 | 18 | 20 | 19 | 19 |
| Number of librarians | 7 | 12 | 29 | 56 | 67 |
| Total library staff other than professional librarians | 16 | 35 | 75 | 176 | 228 |

## Table A.2

## Mean Values of Various Library Statistics for Public Institutions

| | ENROLLMENT | | | | |
|---|---|---|---|---|---|
| | 1,000-2,499 | 2,500-4,999 | 5,000-9,999 | 10,000-19,999 | 20,000+ |
| Total enrollment, 1967 . . . . . . . . . . . . . . . . | 1,737 | 3,682 | 7,257 | 14,482 | 17,992 |
| Volumes held, 1966-67 . . . . . . . . . . . . . . . . | 64,340 | 108,180 | 201,030 | 554,930 | 644,500 |
| Volumes added, 1967-68 . . . . . . . . . . | 8,070 | 14,360 | 23,270 | 52,840 | 59,760 |
| Cost of volumes added . . . . . . . . . . | 57,300 | 119,600 | 179,300 | 414,100 | 485,700 |
| Total library operating costs . . . . . . . . . . | 137,700 | 281,000 | 449,800 | 1,056,100 | 1,345,100 |
| Educational expenditures per student . . . . . . . . . . | 1,410 | 1,211 | 1,191 | 1,670 | 2,065 |
| Percentage of collection in physical sciences, biomedicine, technology . . . . . . . . . . | 25 | 19 | 20 | 23 | 22 |
| Number of librarians . . . . . . . . . . | 4 | 10 | 17 | 37 | 50 |
| Total library staff other than professional librarians . . . . . . . . . . | 10 | 20 | 30 | 67 | 95 |

84

## Table A.3

### Simple Correlation Coefficients among Various Library Statistics for Private Institutions

| | Total Enrollment, 1967 | Volumes Held, 1966-67 | Volumes Added, 1967-68 | Cost of Volumes Added | Total Library Operating Costs | Educational Expenditures per Student | Percentage of Collection in Physical Sciences, Biomedicine, Technology | Number of Librarians | Total Library Staff |
|---|---|---|---|---|---|---|---|---|---|
| Volumes held, 1966-67 | 0.52 | | | | | | | | |
| Volumes added, 1967-68 | 0.68 | 0.91 | | | | | | | |
| Cost of volumes added | 0.69 | 0.87 | 0.96 | | | | | | |
| Total library operating costs | 0.61 | 0.97 | 0.97 | 0.95 | | | | | |
| Educational expenditures per student | 0.18 | 0.45 | 0.52 | 0.56 | 0.52 | | | | |
| Percentage of collection in physical sciences, biomedicine, technology | 0.09 | 0.04 | 0.07 | 0.10 | 0.08 | 0.20 | | | |
| Number of librarians | 0.60 | 0.93 | 0.93 | 0.92 | 0.96 | 0.53 | 0.08 | | |
| Total library staff | 0.58 | 0.86 | 0.88 | 0.86 | 0.90 | 0.47 | 0.05 | 0.91 | |
| Total library staff other than professional librarians | 0.56 | 0.81 | 0.84 | 0.82 | 0.86 | 0.28 | 0.44 | 0.86 | 0.99 |

## Table A.4

## Simple Correlation Coefficients among Various Library Statistics for Public Institutions

| | Total Enrollment, 1967 | Volumes Held, 1966-67 | Volumes Added, 1967-68 | Cost of Volumes Added | Total Library Operating Costs | Educational Expenditures per Student | Percentage of Collection in Physical Sciences, Biomedicine, Technology | Number of Librarians | Total Library Staff |
|---|---|---|---|---|---|---|---|---|---|
| Volumes held, 1966-67 . . . . . . . . . . | 0.75 | | | | | | | | |
| Volumes added, 1967-68 . . . . . . . | 0.80 | 0.80 | | | | | | | |
| Cost of volumes added . . . . . . . . | 0.78 | 0.74 | 0.90 | | | | | | |
| Total library operating costs . . . . . | 0.85 | 0.87 | 0.91 | 0.94 | | | | | |
| Educational expenditures per student . . . . | 0.21 | 0.27 | 0.21 | 0.21 | 0.28 | | | | |
| Percentage of collection in physical sciences, biomedicine, technology . . . . | -0.07 | -0.01 | -0.08 | -0.06 | -0.05 | 0.10 | | | |
| Number of librarians . . . . . . . . . | 0.81 | 0.89 | 0.80 | 0.79 | 0.92 | 0.29 | -0.08 | | |
| Total library staff . . . . . . . . | 0.74 | 0.84 | 0.78 | 0.77 | 0.90 | 0.34 | -0.07 | 0.92 | |
| Total library staff other than professional librarians . . . . . . . . | 0.67 | 0.78 | 0.73 | 0.73 | 0.85 | -0.34 | -0.16 | 0.83 | 0.98 |

## Table A.5

### Regression Results for Private Colleges
### with Enrollments of 1,000-2,499

| EXPLANATORY VARIABLE | DEPENDENT VARIABLE | | | | |
|---|---|---|---|---|---|
| | *Number of Professional Librarians* | *Total Library Staff* | *Volumes Added, 1967-68 (× 10,000)* | *Cost of Volumes Added (× $100,000)* | *Total Library Operating Costs (× $100,000)* |
| Volumes held, 1966-67 (× 10,000) | 0.3716 | 1.4454 | 0.0229 | 0.0125 | 0.0464 |
| *t*-ratio . . . . . . . . . | 8.0949 | 9.8580 | 8.7212 | 7.3166 | 12.6317 |
| Expenditures per student (× $1,000) . | 0.1061 | 0.3344 | 0.0350 | – | – |
| *t*-ratio . . . . . . . . . | 0.4026 | 0.3973 | 2.3195 | – | – |
| Volumes added, 1967-68 (× 10,000) | – | – | – | 0.4946 | 0.9050 |
| *t*-ratio . . . . . . . . . | – | – | – | 13.3206 | 12.5955 |
| Number of professional librarians . . . | – | – | – | – | 0.0139 |
| *t*-ratio . . . . . . . . . | – | – | – | – | 3.3561 |
| Constant term . . . . | 2.6595 | 7.2665 | 0.3970 | −0.0209 | 0.0512 |
| *t*-ratio . . . . . . . . . | 4.7219 | 4.0393 | 12.3206 | −0.8798 | 1.0669 |
| $\overline{R}^2$ . . . . . . . . . . . | 0.2288 | 0.3053 | 0.3023 | 0.6369 | 0.7554 |

*Note:* Definitions of variables can be found in the note to table 2.2 on page 23.

## Table A.6

## Regression Results for Private Colleges
## with Enrollments of 2,500-4,999

| EXPLANATORY VARIABLE | DEPENDENT VARIABLE | | | | |
|---|---|---|---|---|---|
| | Number of Professional Librarians | Total Library Staff | Volumes Added, 1967-68 (× 10,000) | Cost of Volumes Added (× $100,000) | Total Library Operating Costs (× $100,000) |
| Volumes held, 1966-67 (× 10,000) | 0.3258 | 1.5009 | 0.0248 | 0.0186 | 0.0609 |
| t-ratio . . . . . . . . . . | 6.5193 | 5.3382 | 5.4915 | 4.9441 | 6.8161 |
| Expenditures per student (× $1,000) | 3.9027 | 11.5751 | 0.2257 | – | – |
| t-ratio . . . . . . . . . . | 4.8525 | 2.5582 | 3.1003 | – | – |
| Volumes added, 1967-68 (× 10,000) | – | – | – | 0.7962 | 0.7477 |
| t-ratio . . . . . . . . . . | – | – | – | 8.9655 | 3.9546 |
| Number of professional librarians . . . | – | – | – | – | 0.0782 |
| t-ratio . . . . . . . . . . | – | – | – | – | 4.9859 |
| Constant term . . . . | −0.6153 | 0.6744 | 0.4084 | −0.2707 | −0.2258 |
| t-ratio . . . . . . . . . . | −0.6031 | 0.1175 | 4.4232 | −3.5070 | −1.5198 |
| $\overline{R}^2$ . . . . . . . . . . . | 0.8627 | 0.7524 | 0.7821 | 0.9191 | 0.9554 |

*Note:* Definitions of variables can be found in the note to table 2.2 on page 23.

## Table A.7

## Regression Results for Private Colleges
## with Enrollments of 5,000-9,999

| EXPLANATORY VARIABLE | DEPENDENT VARIABLE | | | | |
|---|---|---|---|---|---|
| | Number of Professional Librarians | Total Library Staff | Volumes Added, 1967-68 (× 10,000) | Cost of Volumes Added (× $100,000) | Total Library Operating Costs (× $100,000) |
| Volumes held, 1966-67 (× 10,000) | 0.3378 | 1.1471 | 0.0363 | 0.0191 | 0.0505 |
| $t$-ratio . . . . . . . . . | 5.7098 | 4.3983 | 9.8556 | 4.6885 | 4.3127 |
| Expenditures per student (× $1,000) | 2.0734 | 7.6514 | 0.1292 | – | – |
| $t$-ratio . . . . . . . . . | 3.9235 | 3.2842 | 3.9231 | – | – |
| Volumes added, 1967-68 (× 10,000) | – | – | – | 0.4087 | 0.6849 |
| $t$-ratio . . . . . . . . | – | – | – | 4.9254 | 2.4972 |
| Number of professional librarians . . . | – | – | – | – | 0.0732 |
| $t$-ratio . . . . . . . . | – | – | – | – | 4.2793 |
| Constant term . . . . | 8.1691 | 32.5164 | 0.8431 | 0.2611 | 0.2187 |
| $t$-ratio . . . . . . . . . | 2.7201 | 2.4559 | 4.5029 | 1.9961 | 0.5849 |
| $\bar{R}^2$ . . . . . . . . . . . | 0.7274 | 0.6253 | 0.8527 | 0.9243 | 0.9368 |

*Note:* Definitions of variables can be found in the note to table 2.2 on page 23.

89

## Table A.8

### Regression Results for Private Colleges
### with Enrollments of 10,000-20,000

| EXPLANATORY VARIABLE | DEPENDENT VARIABLE | | | | |
|---|---|---|---|---|---|
| | Number of Professional Librarians | Total Library Staff | Volumes Added, 1967-68 (x 10,000) | Cost of Volumes Added (x $100,000) | Total Library Operating Costs (x $100,000) |
| Volumes held, 1966-67 (x 10,000) | 0.5059 | 3.1531 | 0.0430 | 0.0132 | 0.0493 |
| t-ratio . . . . . . . . . . | 6.8471 | 3.9149 | 4.8789 | 1.6853 | 2.6507 |
| Expenditures per student (x $1,000) | −1.2052 | −17.2125 | −0.0545 | − | − |
| t-ratio . . . . . . . . . . | −0.8096 | −1.0607 | −0.3070 | − | − |
| Volumes added, 1967-68 (x 10,000) | − | − | − | 0.4830 | 0.8175 |
| t-ratio . . . . . . . . . . | − | − | − | 2.7339 | 2.4375 |
| Number of professional librarians . . . | − | − | − | − | 0.1093 |
| t-ratio . . . . . . . . . . | − | − | − | − | 2.7932 |
| Constant term . . . . | 9.5538 | −19.5912 | 2.1800 | 0.4120 | −0.5432 |
| t-ratio . . . . . . . . . . | 1.7301 | −0.3255 | 3.3120 | 0.7215 | −0.5411 |
| $\bar{R}^2$ . . . . . . . . . . . | 0.8894 | 0.6559 | 0.8159 | 0.8844 | 0.9755 |

*Note:* Definitions of variables can be found in the note to table 2.2 on page 23.

## Table A.9

## Regression Results for Public Colleges
### with Enrollments of 1,000-2,499

| EXPLANATORY VARIABLE | DEPENDENT VARIABLE | | | | |
|---|---|---|---|---|---|
| | Number of Professional Librarians | Total Library Staff | Volumes Added, 1967-68 (× 10,000) | Cost of Volumes Added (× $100,000) | Total Library Operating Costs (× $100,000) |
| Volumes held, 1966-67 (× 10,000) | 0.1945 | −0.2708 | 0.0269 | −0.0124 | 0.0293 |
| t-ratio ........... | 1.6223 | −0.3442 | 1.4669 | −1.1543 | 1.7021 |
| Expenditures per student (× $1,000) | 0.1860 | 0.6131 | 0.0337 | − | − |
| t-ratio ........... | 0.9199 | 0.4619 | 1.0899 | − | − |
| Volumes added, 1967-68 (× 10,000) | − | − | − | 0.3954 | 0.6027 |
| t-ratio ........... | − | − | − | 5.4439 | 4.9540 |
| Number of professional librarians ... | − | − | − | − | 0.0932 |
| t-ratio ........... | − | − | − | − | 5.0011 |
| Constant term ..... | 3.0015 | 15.7266 | 0.5868 | 0.3335 | 0.2807 |
| t-ratio ........... | 3.4292 | 2.7374 | 4.3868 | 3.7741 | 1.9592 |
| $\bar{R}^2$ ............. | 0.0292 | −0.0269 | 0.0276 | 0.2984 | 0.5751 |

*Note:* Definitions of variables can be found in the note to table 2.2 on page 23.

91

## Table A.10

## Regression Results for Public Colleges
## with Enrollments of 2,500-4,999

| EXPLANATORY VARIABLE | DEPENDENT VARIABLE | | | | |
|---|---|---|---|---|---|
| | Number of Professional Librarians | Total Library Staff | Volumes Added, 1967-68 (x 10,000) | Cost of Volumes Added (x $100,000) | Total Library Operating Costs (x $100,000) |
| Volumes held, 1966-67 (x 10,000) | 0.4148 | 2.2671 | 0.0990 | −0.0102 | 0.0260 |
| t-ratio ........... | 3.0659 | 3.0610 | 4.8310 | −0.8057 | 1.1667 |
| Expenditures per student (x $1,000) | 1.0555 | 1.3984 | −0.0323 | − | − |
| t-ratio ........... | 2.0156 | 0.4878 | −0.4072 | − | − |
| Volumes added, 1967-68 (x 10,000) | − | − | − | 0.8350 | 1.2566 |
| t-ratio ........... | − | − | − | 12.0912 | 9.4737 |
| Number of professional librarians ... | − | − | − | − | 0.0704 |
| t-ratio ........... | − | − | −` | − | 3.6003 |
| Constant term ..... | 4.3316 | 3.4556 | 0.3896 | 0.1126 | 0.0122 |
| t-ratio ........... | 2.9036 | 0.4231 | 1.7234 | 0.8442 | 0.0516 |
| $\bar{R}^2$ .............. | 0.2166 | 0.1311 | 0.2508 | 0.7201 | 0.7843 |

*Note:* Definitions of variables can be found in the note to table 2.2 on page 23.

## Table A.11

## Regression Results for Public Colleges
## with Enrollments of 5,000-9,999

| EXPLANATORY VARIABLE | DEPENDENT VARIABLE | | | | |
|---|---|---|---|---|---|
| | Number of Professional Librarians | Total Library Staff | Volumes Added, 1967-68 (x 10,000) | Cost of Volumes Added (x $100,000) | Total Library Operating Costs (x $100,000) |
| Volumes held, 1966-67 (x 10,000) | 0.1382 | −0.0432 | 0.0412 | −0.0137 | −0.0068 |
| t-ratio .......... | 1.1774 | −0.0950 | 3.1891 | −1.3613 | −0.3872 |
| Expenditures per student (x $1,000) | 5.0462 | 37.1404 | 0.4557 | − | − |
| t-ratio .......... | 2.4277 | 4.6165 | 1.9915 | − | − |
| Volumes added, 1967-68 (x 10,000) | − | − | − | 0.7751 | 1.0654 |
| t-ratio .......... | − | − | − | 8.7785 | 6.1204 |
| Number of professional librarians ... | − | − | − | − | 0.1125 |
| t-ratio .......... | − | − | − | − | 5.9410 |
| Constant term ..... | 8.4672 | 3.5601 | 0.9568 | 0.2651 | 0.2129 |
| t-ratio .......... | 3.2468 | 0.3527 | 3.3331 | 1.1430 | 0.5089 |
| $\overline{R}^2$ .............. | 0.1312 | 0.2482 | 0.2485 | 0.5109 | 0.6694 |

*Note:* Definitions of variables can be found in the note to table 2.2 on page 23.

## Table A.12

### Regression Results for Public Colleges with Enrollments of 10,000-20,000

| EXPLANATORY VARIABLE | DEPENDENT VARIABLE | | | | |
|---|---|---|---|---|---|
| | *Number of Professional Librarians* | *Total Library Staff* | *Volumes Added, 1967-68 (x 10,000)* | *Cost of Volumes Added (x $100,000)* | *Total Library Operating Costs (x $100,000)* |
| Volumes held, 1966-67 (x 10,000) | 0.5017 | 1.2095 | 0.0530 | 0.0185 | 0.0139 |
| *t*-ratio . . . . . . . . . . | 6.1896 | 5.2880 | 3.9557 | 2.5034 | 0.8003 |
| Expenditures per student (x $1,000) | −3.0781 | −0.2633 | −0.3359 | − | − |
| *t*-ratio . . . . . . . . . . | −0.9451 | −0.0286 | −0.6235 | − | − |
| Volumes added, 1967-68 (x 10,000) | − | − | − | 0.4927 | 0.8139 |
| *t*-ratio . . . . . . . . . . | − | − | − | 4.8356 | 4.3756 |
| Number of professional librarians . . . | − | − | − | − | 0.1317 |
| *t*-ratio . . . . . . . . . . | − | − | − | − | 4.3132 |
| Constant term . . . . . | 14.7724 | 37.9067 | 2.9018 | 0.5114 | 0.5571 |
| *t*-ratio . . . . . . . . . . | 3.1951 | 2.9052 | 3.7945 | 1.1058 | 0.6520 |
| $\bar{R}^2$ . . . . . . . . . . . . . | 0.6312 | 0.6025 | 0.3971 | 0.7008 | 0.8420 |

*Note:* Definitions of variables can be found in the note to table 2.2 on page 23.

## Table A.13

### Regression Results for Private Colleges with Enrollments of 2,500-4,999 with Effect of Classification as College Added

| EXPLANATORY VARIABLE | DEPENDENT VARIABLE | | | | |
|---|---|---|---|---|---|
| | Number of Professional Librarians | Total Library Staff | Volumes Added, 1967-68 (× 10,000) | Cost of Volumes Added (× $100,000) | Total Library Operating Costs (× $100,000) |
| Volumes held, 1966-67 (× 10,000) | 0.3416 | 1.5347 | 0.0258 | 0.0192 | 0.0637 |
| $t$-ratio .......... | 7.1272 | 5.4191 | 5.7403 | 5.4497 | 6.8409 |
| Expenditures per student (× $1,000) | 2.8771 | 9.3799 | 0.1658 | – | – |
| $t$-ratio .......... | 3.3788 | 1.8643 | 2.0791 | – | – |
| Volumes added, 1967-68 (× 10,000) | – | – | – | 0.7051 | 0.7147 |
| $t$-ratio .......... | – | – | – | 7.9546 | 3.7351 |
| Number of professional librarians ... | – | – | – | – | 0.0711 |
| $t$-ratio .......... | – | – | – | – | 4.1714 |
| Effect of classification as college[a].. | –6.9845 | –14.9500 | –0.4080 | –0.5047 | –0.3898 |
| $t$-ratio .......... | –2.7548 | –0.9979 | –1.7186 | –3.0618 | –1.0677 |
| Constant term ..... | 6.9417 | 16.8499 | 0.8498 | 0.2747 | 0.1895 |
| $t$-ratio .......... | 2.3853 | 0.9799 | 3.1190 | 1.4283 | 0.4552 |
| $\bar{R}^2$ ............. | 0.8755 | 0.7524 | 0.7886 | 0.9285 | 0.9555 |

*Note:* Definitions of variables can be found in the note to table 2.2 on page 23.

[a]Institutions were classified as universities if they (1) give considerable emphasis to graduate instruction, (2) award advanced degrees as well as baccalaureates in a variety of liberal arts fields, and (3) have at least two professional schools that are not exclusively technological. All other four-year institutions of higher education were classified as colleges.

## Table A.14

## Regression Results for Private Colleges with Enrollments of 5,000-9,999 with Effect of Classification as College Added

| EXPLANATORY VARIABLE | DEPENDENT VARIABLE | | | | |
|---|---|---|---|---|---|
| | Number of Professional Librarians | Total Library Staff | Volumes Added, 1967-68 (× 10,000) | Cost of Volumes Added (× $100,000) | Total Library Operating Costs (× $100,000) |
| Volumes held, 1966-67 (× 10,000) | 0.3766 | 1.1404 | 0.0366 | 0.0205 | 0.0496 |
| $t$-ratio .......... | 6.0828 | 4.0017 | 9.0949 | 5.0692 | 4.0505 |
| Expenditures per student (× $1,000) | 2.1515 | 7.6379 | 0.1298 | – | – |
| $t$-ratio .......... | 4.1693 | 3.2157 | 3.8671 | – | – |
| Volumes added, 1967-68 (× 10,000) | – | – | – | 0.4118 | 0.6729 |
| $t$-ratio .......... | – | – | – | 5.1020 | 2.3956 |
| Number of professional librarians ... | – | – | – | – | 0.0744 |
| $t$-ratio .......... | – | – | – | – | 4.1769 |
| Effect of classification as college[a] . | 7.7879 | −1.3467 | 0.0572 | 0.2798 | −0.1551 |
| $t$-ratio .......... | 1.6983 | −0.0638 | 0.1916 | 1.7025 | −0.3089 |
| Constant term ..... | 3.2445 | 33.3680 | 0.8069 | 0.0825 | 0.3156 |
| $t$-ratio .......... | 0.7883 | 1.7614 | 3.0137 | 0.5003 | 0.6413 |
| $\bar{R}^2$ .............. | 0.7421 | 0.6136 | 0.8483 | 0.9284 | 0.9349 |

*Note:* Definitions of variables can be found in the note to table 2.2 on page 23.

[a]Institutions were classified as universities if they (1) give considerable emphasis to graduate instruction, (2) award advanced degrees as well as baccalaureates in a variety of liberal arts fields, and (3) have at least two professional schools that are not exclusively technological. All other four-year institutions of higher education were classified as colleges.

## Table A.15

### Regression Results for Public Colleges with Enrollments of 5,000-9,999 with Effect of Classification as College Added

| EXPLANATORY VARIABLE | DEPENDENT VARIABLE | | | | |
|---|---|---|---|---|---|
| | Number of Professional Librarians | Total Library Staff | Volumes Added, 1967-68 (x 10,000) | Cost of Volumes Added (x $100,000) | Total Library Operating Costs (x $100,000) |
| Volumes held, 1966-67 (x 10,000) | 0.1195 | 0.4302 | 0.0528 | −0.0260 | −0.0225 |
| t-ratio .......... | 0.9259 | 0.8914 | 3.8130 | −2.1127 | −1.0393 |
| Expenditures per student (x $1,000) | 4.4638 | 51.9419 | 0.8193 | – | – |
| t-ratio .......... | 1.6806 | 5.2317 | 2.8748 | – | – |
| Volumes added, 1967-68 (x 10,000) | – | – | – | 0.7810 | 1.0983 |
| t-ratio .......... | – | – | – | 8.9428 | 6.2562 |
| Number of professional librarians ... | – | – | – | – | 0.1068 |
| t-ratio .......... | – | – | – | – | 5.4903 |
| Effect of classification as college[a].. | −1.7817 | 45.2847 | 1.1125 | −0.5883 | −0.7668 |
| t-ratio .......... | −0.3553 | 2.4160 | 2.0677 | −1.7019 | −1.2316 |
| Constant term ..... | 11.0161 | −61.2262 | −0.6348 | 0.9865 | 1.1881 |
| t-ratio .......... | 1.4423 | −2.1444 | −0.7746 | 2.0472 | 1.3276 |
| $\bar{R}^2$ .............. | 0.1216 | 0.2910 | 0.2780 | 0.5222 | 0.6715 |

*Note:* Definitions of variables can be found in the note to table 2.2 on page 23.

[a]Institutions were classified as universities if they (1) give considerable emphasis to graduate instruction, (2) award advanced degrees as well as baccalaureates in a variety of liberal arts fields, and (3) have at least two professional schools that are not exclusively technological. All other four-year institutions of higher education were classified as colleges.

## Regression Results for Public Colleges with Enrollments of 10,000-20,000 with Effect of Classification as College Added

| EXPLANATORY VARIABLE | DEPENDENT VARIABLE | | | | |
|---|---|---|---|---|---|
| | Number of Professional Librarians | Total Library Staff | Volumes Added, 1967-68 (× 10,000) | Cost of Volumes Added (× $100,000) | Total Library Operating Costs (× $100,000) |
| Volumes held, 1966-67 (× 10,000) | 0.5245 | 1.2483 | 0.0575 | 0.0216 | 0.0159 |
| t-ratio .......... | 6.0475 | 5.0685 | 4.0273 | 2.3791 | 0.7676 |
| Expenditures per student (× $1,000) | −2.3477 | 0.9804 | −0.1919 | − | − |
| t-ratio .......... | −0.6883 | 0.1012 | −0.3415 | − | − |
| Volumes added, 1967-68 (× 10,000) | − | − | − | 0.4808 | 0.8086 |
| t-ratio .......... | − | − | − | 4.5839 | 4.2268 |
| Number of professional librarians ... | − | − | − | − | 0.1309 |
| t-ratio .......... | − | − | − | − | 4.1779 |
| Effect of classification as college[a] . | 4.7928 | 8.1612 | 0.9452 | 0.3448 | 0.1906 |
| t-ratio .......... | 0.7746 | 0.4644 | 0.9274 | 0.6006 | 0.1854 |
| Constant term ..... | 10.7370 | 31.0351 | 2.1060 | 0.2911 | 0.4420 |
| t-ratio .......... | 1.5370 | 1.5644 | 1.8304 | 0.4900 | 0.4139 |
| $\bar{R}^2$ .............. | 0.6264 | 0.5921 | 0.3944 | 0.6945 | 0.8368 |

*Note:* Definitions of variables can be found in the note to table 2.2 on page 23.

[a]Institutions were classified as universities if they (1) give considerable emphasis to graduate instruction, (2) award advanced degrees as well as baccalaureates in a variety of liberal arts fields, and (3) have at least two professional schools that are not exclusively technological. All other four-year institutions of higher education were classified as colleges.

## COUNCIL ON LIBRARY RESOURCES

Fred C. Cole, *President*

The Council on Library Resources was established in 1956 with support from the Ford Foundation, from which it continues to derive its funding. The Council is a private operating foundation which, through directly administered programs as well as grants to, and contracts with, other organizations, seeks to aid in the solution of problems of libraries generally and of academic and research libraries in particular.

# AMERICAN COUNCIL ON EDUCATION

Roger W. Heyns, *President*

The American Council on Education, founded in 1918, is a council of educational organizations and institutions. Its purpose is to advance education and educational methods through comprehensive voluntary and cooperative action on the part of educational associations, organizations, and institutions.